MARRIAGE
AND DIVORCE

Other Books in the Current Controversies Series:

MARRIAGE AND DIVORCE

David Bender, *Publisher*
Bruno Leone, *Executive Editor*

Scott Barbour, *Managing Editor*
Brenda Stalcup, *Senior Editor*

Tamara L. Roleff, *Book Editor*
Mary E. Williams, *Book Editor*

CURRENT CONTROVERSIES

Library of Congress Cataloging-in-Publication Data

Marriage and divorce / Tamara L. Roleff, Mary E. Williams, book editors.
    p. cm. — (Current controversies)
    Includes bibliographical references and index.
    ISBN 1-56510-568-0 (lib. : alk. paper). — ISBN 1-56510-567-2
(pbk. : alk. paper)
    1. Marriage—United States. 2. Divorce—United States. 3. Gay
marriage—United States. I. Roleff, Tamara L., 1959–   . II. Williams,
Mary E., 1960–   . III. Series.
HQ536.M324   1997
306.81'0973—dc21   97-4941
                                                                        CIP

© 1997 by Greenhaven Press, Inc., PO Box 289009, San Diego, CA 92198-9009
Printed in the U.S.A.

Contents

Chapter 1: What Measures Would Strengthen Marriage?

Chapter 2: Is Divorce Harmful?

Yes: Divorce Is Harmful

No: Divorce Is Not Always Harmful

Many commentators have exaggerated the harmful effects of marital breakups on children. Contrary to the claims of the antidivorce movement, many children of divorce are psychologically healthy and well-adjusted, and many divorced parents fulfill their economic and emotional obligations to their children.

Chapter 3: How Should Society Address the Issues of Divorce and Child Custody?

Chapter 4: Should Gay Marriage Be Legalized?

No: Gay Marriage Should Not Be Legalized

Foreword

By definition, controversies are "discussions of questions in which opposing opinions clash" (Webster's Twentieth Century Dictionary Unabridged). Few would deny that controversies are a pervasive part of the human condition and exist on virtually every level of human enterprise. Controversies transpire between individuals and among groups, within nations and between nations. Controversies supply the grist necessary for progress by providing challenges and challengers to the status quo. They also create atmospheres where strife and warfare can flourish. A world without controversies would be a peaceful world; but it also would be, by and large, static and prosaic.

The Series' Purpose

The purpose of the Current Controversies series is to explore many of the social, political, and economic controversies dominating the national and international scenes today. Titles selected for inclusion in the series are highly focused and specific. For example, from the larger category of criminal justice, Current Controversies deals with specific topics such as police brutality, gun control, white collar crime, and others. The debates in Current Controversies also are presented in a useful, timeless fashion. Articles and book excerpts included in each title are selected if they contribute valuable, long-range ideas to the overall debate. And wherever possible, current information is enhanced with historical documents and other relevant materials. Thus, while individual titles are current in focus, every effort is made to ensure that they will not become quickly outdated. Books in the Current Controversies series will remain important resources for librarians, teachers, and students for many years.

In addition to keeping the titles focused and specific, great care is taken in the editorial format of each book in the series. Book introductions and chapter prefaces are offered to provide background material for readers. Chapters are organized around several key questions that are answered with diverse opinions representing all points on the political spectrum. Materials in each chapter include opinions in which authors clearly disagree as well as alternative opinions in which authors may agree on a broader issue but disagree on the possible solutions. In this way, the content of each volume in Current Controversies mirrors the mosaic of opinions encountered in society. Readers will quickly realize that there are many viable answers to these complex issues. By questioning each author's conclusions, students and casual readers can begin to develop the critical thinking skills so important to evaluating opinionated material.

Current Controversies is also ideal for controlled research. Each anthology in the series is composed of primary sources taken from a wide gamut of informational categories including periodicals, newspapers, books, United States and foreign government documents, and the publications of private and public organizations. Readers will find factual support for reports, debates, and research papers covering all areas of important issues. In addition, an annotated table of contents, an index, a book and periodical bibliography, and a list of organizations to contact are included in each book to expedite further research.

Perhaps more than ever before in history, people are confronted with diverse and contradictory information. During the Persian Gulf War, for example, the public was not only treated to minute-to-minute coverage of the war, it was also inundated with critiques of the coverage and countless analyses of the factors motivating U.S. involvement. Being able to sort through the plethora of opinions accompanying today's major issues, and to draw one's own conclusions, can be a complicated and frustrating struggle. It is the editors' hope that Current Controversies will help readers with this struggle.

"The impact that changing divorce laws will have on the divorce rate is debatable."

Introduction

The United States has consistently led the world in the number of marriages each year, with a marriage rate roughly twice as high as those in other industrialized countries. It has also consistently led the world in the divorce rate. During the 1960s, the divorce rate in the United States began to climb rapidly. In 1960, there were nine divorces for every thousand married women; by 1970, the number had shot up to fifteen per thousand. Divorces peaked in 1980 at twenty-three per thousand and have since leveled off at twenty-one per thousand married women in the early 1990s.

Concerned about the country's high divorce rate, clergy, academics, sociologists, politicians, and others have called for measures to slow it down. One proposal is to return to fault-based divorce, which was the law of the land prior to 1969. Divorce then was granted only in specific circumstances, generally limited to infidelity, physical or mental cruelty, or desertion. Couples who wished to divorce had to prove in court that one spouse was solely responsible for the breakdown of the marriage. Only the innocent party was allowed to sue for divorce, thus ensuring that all divorces granted were consented to by both spouses. If one spouse did not want a divorce and was not guilty of any transgression, a divorce would not be granted. If both partners were found guilty of fault, they were deemed to deserve each other and no divorce was granted.

California's no-fault divorce statute, signed into law in 1969 by then-governor Ronald Reagan, started a cultural revolution that saw forty-four states adopting no-fault divorce within the next five years, and all fifty states adopting it by 1984. With the advent of no-fault divorce, married couples did not have to prove who was responsible for the broken marriage. A divorce could be granted based solely on incompatibility or the irretrievable breakdown of the marriage.

Opponents of no-fault divorce contend that the relaxed rules concerning divorce are behind the nation's high divorce rate. When a divorce is easy to obtain, they claim, it is easier to dissolve a marriage than it is to try to repair it. No-fault divorce foes cite a 1995 study in the *Journal of*

Marriage and the Family that found that the divorce rate increased between 15 and 25 percent in the three years following the adoption of no-fault divorce laws.

No-fault divorce also allows one spouse to dissolve a marriage at any time for any reason—or for no reason at all—regardless of the wishes of the other spouse, opponents assert. The ability to make such a unilateral decision abrogates the marriage contract, contends Lenore Weitzman, author of *The Divorce Revolution*. She maintains that no-fault divorce transforms marriage into a "time-limited contingent arrangement rather than a lifelong commitment." No-fault divorce laws also give all the power to the spouse who wants to get divorced, she asserts, thus "elevat[ing] one's 'right' to a divorce over a spouse's 'right' to remain married." What society must do, Weitzman concludes, is return to the strengths of fault-based divorce, in which the law protects the spouse who remains true to the marriage contract rather than blessing the one who wants to break it.

Supporters of no-fault divorce argue that changing the law will not necessarily lower the number of divorces. As Hanna Rosin writes in the May 6, 1996, issue of the *New Republic,* "Correlation does not prove causation." She maintains that the American divorce rate has been rising since the 1800s and almost doubled between 1960 and 1970, years before most states had adopted no-fault divorce laws. "The sudden spike in the three years following the reform came from a backlog of cases," Rosin claims, and was merely a response to changes in America's culture brought on by the sexual revolution. Returning to fault-based divorce would not result in a lower divorce rate or make marriages last longer, she contends.

In addition, a return to fault-based divorce would hurt the families it is trying to protect, no-fault supporters argue. According to Constance Ahrons, author of *The Good Divorce* and director of the marriage and family-therapy program at the University of Southern California, "When one spouse must prove the other to be 'at fault,' divorce becomes a pitched battle between adversaries who each must prove the other committed adultery, spousal abuse or child abuse or destroyed the home. . . . Anger escalates and continues for years or decades following the divorce." Furthermore, she contends, litigation in fault-based divorces harms the children who are forced to watch their parents battle in a long, vicious war. No-fault divorce reduces the acrimony, she maintains, and provides a "civilized arena in which marriage can be terminated while parents continue to be parents."

The impact that changing divorce laws would have on the divorce rate is debatable. Both sides of the no-fault divorce issue recognize the importance of marriage and family; however, each believes its approach to divorce is the best way to preserve the family and protect both the parents and the children. *Marriage and Divorce: Current Controversies* examines this issue as well as the debate over whether divorce is harmful, whether divorce laws and child custody should be reformed, whether homosexuals should be allowed to marry, and how marriage can be strengthened.

Chapter 1

What Measures Would Strengthen Marriage?

CURRENT CONTROVERSIES

Chapter Preface

Living together before marriage is becoming more and more common among dating couples. According to the U.S. Census Bureau, more than 3.7 million unmarried opposite-sex partners were living together in 1994. One of the most frequently heard reasons for living together before marriage is that the arrangement is a kind of trial marriage to see if the relationship will last. Critics of pre marital cohabitation charge, however, that living together before marriage does not prepare a couple for the reality of marriage. They cite studies that show, in fact, that couples who live together before marriage are 33 to 80 percent more likely to divorce than are couples who do not cohabitate before marriage. Opponents of premarital cohabitation also contend that the longer a couple lives together before marriage the more likely it is that their marriage will end in divorce.

However, some researchers maintain that in order to correctly interpret these study results, characteristics of the research subjects should be taken into consideration. James Sweet, a researcher and the author of a study that found couples who cohabitated before marriage were 33 percent more likely to divorce, explains that "the *type* of people who live together are likely to experience more marital disruption." According to Sweet, people who live together prior to marriage generally come from large cities and grow up in broken homes, are less romantic and religious, and are more impatient when things go wrong. These traits are found more frequently in people who divorce, Sweet maintains, regardless of whether they have cohabitated before marriage.

Premarital cohabitation is a controversial issue in the debate about marriage and divorce. In the following chapter, the authors examine this and other measures that may strengthen marriage, both as an institution and on a personal level.

Premarital Cohabitation Can Strengthen Marriage

by Kerry Danner

About the author: *Kerry Danner is a freelance writer in Arlington, Virginia.*

A few years ago when friends Ted and Nikki started PreCana [a program that prepares engaged Catholic couples for marriage], they decided against telling the priest that they were living together. One night, as they took part in a marriage preparation exercise with other engaged couples, that conflict came to a head.

A group of about 10 couples sat around in a circle with a priest and a sponsoring married couple. In the middle was a hatful of small pieces of paper, each proposing a hypothetical scenario involving "your future spouse."

Each person had to draw from the hat and, using their imagination and problem-solving skills, respond to the scenario described. As Nikki told the story, she picked a paper out of the hat, read it and looked at Ted terrified.

She vaguely remembers that the scenario had to do with living with your partner. She stood up and started to cry, "I can't go on with it! We are living together; OK, we live together." Two or three other couples stood up saying, "It's OK, it's OK. We live together, too," thereby transforming the PreCana event into a therapy session for Catholics who cohabitate.

Living Together Makes Sense

I, like many of my peers, live with a partner to whom I am deeply committed. My choice to live with Jay, my fiancé, before marriage came out of deep love and respect for him. Our individual work schedules were busy, we lived an hour's drive apart and missed each other greatly. We had long before spoken the marriage vows to each other.

Living together made economic sense, too. But perhaps, even more, we choose to live together because there is something so wonderful about sleeping—and I do mean just sleeping—wrapped in someone's arms. Moving in together was as natural to us as was the decision to get married.

Not long ago, Jay and I attended a Catholic Engaged Encounter weekend as

From Kerry Danner, "Hello, My Name Is Kerry, and I Live in Sin," *National Catholic Reporter*, May 3, 1996. Reprinted by permission of the author.

part of our PreCana instruction. During the weekend, we spoke with several couples and the program's hosts about the reasons some couples choose to misrepresent their living situations. One of the host couples, John and Regina Keegan, Engaged Encounter coordinators for the Arlington, Va., diocese, told us that, as a rule of thumb, five couples on a 30-couple weekend actually write on their forms that they live together.

Jay and I spoke personally with at least three couples on our weekend who live together and, out of fear of harassment or judgment, listed separate addresses on the form.

> *"There are times when living with a partner can be a wonderful and helpful option for a committed couple before their ceremony."*

Fear of rejection by family members and church leaders seems to be the most pervasive motivation for couples to hide a decision to live together. The mother of one of my friends has threatened to refuse to pay for her wedding if she lives with her fiancé before marriage. John Keegan knew one woman who had a separate telephone line installed in the home she shared with her fiancé so her mother would not know they lived together. As Jay and I spoke with couples, many were hesitant to talk about their situations when the host couples were in the room.

Regina Keegan believes that many people are afraid to be honest about their living arrangements because they still perceive the church to be judging and don't want to be singled out. Although Regina says a couple's living situation is their business, and the host couples are not there to judge, there are enough horror stories about critical priests or unforgiving parents around to make any rational person think twice before filling out PreCana papers.

Rejected by the Church

Three years ago, a friend and her then-fiancé who lived together approached their parish priest to inquire about starting PreCana. They, too, had already vowed to spend their lives together before they approached the priest. Yet, when they did, they were told they were not worthy of receiving the sacrament. The priest acknowledged that he knew many couples lived together to save money. But he said they could find other ways to save. For instance, they could forgo a big, fancy wedding. Or, he suggested, they could seek a secular wedding, and he could "bless" them in the sacristy.

The priest went on to complain about "those" young couples who live together and then insist on having seven limousines in front of St. Patrick's. (You have no right to openly celebrate your wedding and life commitment if you've already had sex?)

They came into his office happy and confident in their love, and left infuriated. Eventually, they were able to get married by a more compassionate priest. Since then, they have distanced themselves from the church.

I know of at least two other couples who, when honest about living together, were told by their priest they'd have to move into separate homes or he couldn't marry them. These couples chose not to get married in the Catholic church at all.

We are fostering an unhealthy dependency on the hierarchy when we allow such incidents to occur. Yet, if a couple feels they have been treated unfairly or have been harassed and demoralized, where can they go? It saddens me to think of the church attacking couples with angry and judging words, particularly as these couples may be setting life patterns. I question whether the church community wants couples to be made to feel ashamed of their decisions or encouraged to lie.

As I was growing up Catholic, I was constantly informed by my parents, parochial school teachers and priests of the church's teachings on premarital sex and cohabitation, and I acknowledge I am in conflict with it. I agree with the view that it is unwise, if not immoral, to live with someone prior to expressing a mutual commitment. I would hope that every couple would seriously reflect on and discuss the implications of living together before deciding to do so.

A Wonderful Option

I do not, however, understand why church communities continue to refuse to acknowledge that there are times when living with a partner can be a wonderful and helpful option for a committed couple before their ceremony.

Society and relationships within it have changed so much that living together and being married have taken on new meaning. A divorce rate of 50 percent is pretty intimidating to any young couple starting off. More and more people recognize that the real strength and lasting character of the marriage comes, not from the papers or the ceremony, but from the deep love, loyalty and maturity that a couple shares.

As confident as Jay and I are in our love, it took us almost five months to work up the courage to go talk to a "priest," not because we didn't want to get married in the church, but because we were afraid and angry. I

> *"Living together makes us better able to love each other, our friends, families and communities."*

knew that if a priest told us that we were "sinners" and encouraged us to move into separate places, my anger might force me to leave the church altogether.

I was also angry at myself for even wondering if Jay and I should lie about our situation. I didn't want to hide the fact that I live with Jay. He's my best friend, and we give each other so much strength.

Living together makes us better able to love each other, our friends, families and communities. True love is sparse enough as it is.

Premarital Cohabitation Does Not Strengthen Marriage

by Jo McGowan

About the author: *Jo McGowan is a freelance writer.*

For a person with a lot of friends, I've attended remarkably few weddings. Many of the people I know—white, middle-class, college-educated, liberal or left wing—have chosen to live together instead.

"Why spoil a good thing?" is how one woman puts it. But for most people it's just a way of hedging their bets. In a country where nearly half of all marriages end in divorce, people want to be absolutely sure before making that final commitment.

For those who still believe in the concept of marriage at all, living together is a kind of test run; and to the consumerist mind, which is what most of us have these days, it makes good sense. People don't buy a car without taking it out for a spin first, do they? How can a person possibly leave the choice of a life partner to chance? Living together before marriage is the only way to be sure that the marriage itself will work.

There is, however, a fundamental fallacy in this argument, which in the age of divorce makes it difficult to appreciate. A 50 percent failure rate notwithstanding, the essence of marriage is a permanent commitment. Living together tells a couple precisely nothing about marriage because living together offers neither the rigor nor the comfort of the real thing.

Not the Real Thing

When I was in high school, I used to baby-sit a lot. I loved the children I took care of, and they loved me. I was an expert at changing diapers, settling squabbles, and getting tired kids to bed. I thought that I knew exactly what motherhood was all about and was well prepared to be one when the time came. But,

From Jo McGowan, "There's No Such Thing as a Trial Marriage," *U.S. Catholic*, December 1992. Reprinted with permission from *U.S. Catholic*, published by Claretian Publications, 205 W. Monroe St., Chicago, IL 60606.

in fact, my experience was only two dimensional; and it wasn't until I had my own children that I realized how superficial my involvement had been. Real motherhood is not something a person can walk away from as I could my baby-sitting job.

Now that I am a mother, I know about 3 a.m. fevers and 5 a.m. feeds. I am the one who plays with my children when I would rather read a book and cares that they do their homework and brush their teeth. I am also the one whom they love as they love no one else. The love I shared with my baby-sitting charges was simply an-other species altogether. It was there, and it was wonderful; but it was no match for this.

> *"The permanent commitment that a couple makes on their wedding day . . . is the only way the relationship can grow."*

Living together is similarly just a shadowlike version of marriage. The perma-nent commitment that a couple makes on their wedding day is not simply a nice idea—it is the only way the relationship can grow.

It is worth considering why so few live-in arrangements eventually lead to successful marriages. More often than not, the partnership collapses under its own weight: two people intent on sharing everything need the solid framework of a centuries-old institution to support them. Living together is just too flimsy.

This is not mere sentiment; it is a fact. Marriage, publicly established and wit-nessed by family and friends, is a community event from the start. Couples who choose to marry, recite their vows in the presence of others, and ask those oth-ers to bless their commitment are saying that their lives find meaning in com-munity. However, couples who live together are saying quite the reverse.

What are family and friends to make of it when two people suddenly move in with each other? Typically it is done without ceremony or even announcement. People are left to figure it out on their own. The message is clear: this is our business; leave us alone.

A Radical Difference

Living together differs radically from marriage because it is essentially indi-vidualistic. As such, it requires enormous inner resources to make it work. Peo-ple who marry, on the other hand, take for granted the interest of the commu-nity in seeing that their relationships are a success. The community for its part traditionally encourages the new couple to see themselves as the beginnings of a new unit of society. They are teased and prodded into starting a family; and when their children are born, the community welcomes them with pride be-cause their own ranks are swelled. If a couple runs into a rough patch, family members are sure to do what they can to help work things out. In close-knit so-cieties—as in many ethnic enclaves—enormous efforts are made to keep cou-ples together.

People who live together are usually on their own. Their families, particularly their parents, feel hurt and excluded by their private decisions and quite at a loss to understand their roles vis-à-vis their child's partner. Grandchildren, though often warmly and gracefully received, are a bit of an embarrassment and a dilemma as "relatives" struggle to define themselves in relation to people the law does not recognize as their own. And couples having difficulties are often subtly pressured not to bother working things out. No one expected it to last anyway, is the unspoken message. Parents, in particular, may feel genuine relief as the arrangement seems to be breaking up. At last, they feel, their child can settle down and get married.

People who live together don't even have words for who they are to each other. One can hardly go around saying "This is my lover" when introducing his or her partner (say to an elderly relative or a teacher from third grade)—as if one did nothing but have sex all day long. Anyone who stops to think about it knows this isn't true; but the paucity of language, at least polite language, for this situation should tell us something. When we hear of a couple living together, we tend to think of them in sexual terms; and the reason is simple: people who live together are basically doing it for sex.

If it were just a question of liking each other's company or wanting to save on rent, they could be roommates. If they wanted to build a life together, they could get married. But roommate-hood is too little and marriage is too much. The middle road is living together, and the crucial element is sex.

> *"There is no such thing as a trial marriage."*

Married couples, on the other hand, although clearly engaging in sexual relations, are not perceived in this way. The reason is that marriage itself is a state of life with substance; and people who marry, unless flagrantly irresponsible, inherit as their own the respect given to the institution. Sex is at its core; but it is sex with all its power intact, extending into the future, through both the lifetime promises that husband and wife make to each other and, more concretely, in the children created by its expression.

Not a Trial Marriage

Living together as an insurance policy against making the wrong decision in marriage is a sham. There is no such thing as a trial marriage—just as there is no such thing as trial parenthood. People may take care of someone else's children from morning till night, but nothing on earth can prepare a person for that moment when that person realizes that this baby is his or hers. The surge of love and the terror of responsibility occur simultaneously, and they leave a person breathless.

So, too, with marriage. No other human relationship can duplicate its conditions, and the fact that it is forever makes it both difficult to sustain and possible to accomplish. People need the luxury of a lifetime for the work and love; and being human, people need the security of knowing that they have it. Believing in trial marriage is like people believing they can test the waters without getting their feet wet.

Marriage implies courage, openness, and saying yes to life. And living together? It's a little sad, really: it's to look at life in all its richness and depth and say, "Well, maybe."

Prenuptial Contracts Strengthen Marriage

by Meredith Gould Ruch

About the author: *Meredith Gould Ruch is a freelance journalist and therapist.*

We'd been married just six months, but the atmosphere in our home was already dark with dispute, disappointment, and the fallout of prior marriages. We were such a decent, loving couple, I couldn't believe the cloud cover we'd managed to generate.

My husband turned to me one morning after our zillionth inane argument and announced it was time to get into therapy. I said flatly, "No way." He responded with one word that overruled me: "Contract."

The Premarital Contract

Before we got married, my husband and I had agreed that we would get outside help for our relationship if either of us felt we needed it. This was just one condition of a written agreement that we had the foresight to create in advance of exchanging vows. Our marital agreement represents a consensus we had already reached. The purpose was to provide a vehicle to resolve any future confrontation. I had no choice the morning my husband called for therapy. I joined him in the search for a therapist who, by the way, soon got us back on track.

Every partner brings to marriage a set of values—and strong views—about appropriate roles and behaviors. Ideally, these attitudes move from background to foreground during courtship as we explore with our prospective partner how we feel about such things as sex, money, work, children, in-laws, and chores. Oftentimes, though, the marriage "contract" is not explicit, and conflicts inevitably arise: "You never told me you hated cooking." "Who decided I'd do all the yardwork?" "When did we decide to watch television during dinner?"

My husband and I decided to address these kinds of questions at the outset of our marriage (the second for each of us). We knew we didn't want a contract that read like a list of hostage demands. Nor were we interested in a legally-binding agreement that coldly divided our financial assets in advance. We

Excerpted with permission from "Prenuptial Agreements Make Happier Marriages," by Meredith Gould Ruch, *Natural Health*, September/October 1993. For a trial issue of *Natural Health*, call 1-800-526-8440.

wanted to blend romance with pragmatism, without being too nit-picky or legalistic. We wanted tangible evidence of our shared beliefs.

One night we holed up at home, fortified with plenty of popcorn and chocolate, and we worked out a set of "conditions" and "preferences." What we created was a statement of guiding principles for living our lives together. In addition to a few standard clauses about sexual exclusivity and joint decision-making, we drafted others that express who we are and who we hope to become. Any couple planning marriage can create an agreement that addresses whatever they decide is important to their marriage. Here are the conditions of our agreement that so far have played a role in building a successful marriage.

The Conditions

The well-being of our relationship will always come first.

If there's one fundamental condition, this is it. Each time we put our relationship first, we enhance the "us" we've created through marriage. Choices get simple when we practice this. Over time we've gotten better at letting go of anything that conflicts with the welfare of our marriage. For example:

• My first husband ended our marriage in part because I chose post-graduate work over him. This time, I decided to at least postpone taking a demanding course of study, because it would have taken a lot of time from the first year of my marriage.

• Preserving the well-being of our marriage sometimes calls for us to do things separately. Once, instead of joining me on a trip and being miserable, my husband stayed home and puttered around the house. The time apart gave our marriage the fresh air it needed.

• We blended bank accounts, because building trust was more important to us than having financial autonomy.

• Having separate hair dryers absolutely supports the well-being of our relationship.

We've used this principle to sort through such issues as whom to invite for a weekend, where to stay when visiting relatives, and even how to divide dessert. I believe we have a built-in protection against putting our individual welfare above the health of our partnership.

We are willing to try anything with each other at least once.

My husband insisted we include this provision. I've claimed that I never agreed to it, which irks him to no end. A homebody at heart, my husband is adventuresome in a Walter Mitty-

> *"Any couple planning marriage can create an agreement that addresses whatever they decide is important to their marriage."*

esque way, which is to say, in his head. Nevertheless, I worried about being forced into activities I couldn't veto. I had tried plenty of adventures in the 1970s that I wasn't about to try ever again, even—or perhaps especially—with my husband. My fear faded once I realized we made this condition primarily to experiment with food, rather than try anything kinky or illegal.

To my surprise and his initial horror, I'm the one who may invoke this agreement first. We have an opportunity to live in a spiritual, co-housing community for a year, and I think I want to do it. My husband thinks he does, too, but having never tried it before, he's understandably nervous. I haven't quite said "contract" yet, but I just might.

Now I understand why he wanted this included—it promotes adventure in a safely contained way and opens up possibilities we might not otherwise consider.

Additional Rules

We will go to sleep with as much completion as possible.

Lots of couples have a "never go to sleep angry" rule. We realized how absurd this was after arguing all night, then collapsing into bed with nothing resolved. We also realized that rushing to end a dispute by bedtime—as if we'd turn into pumpkins otherwise—usually creates a false sense of resolution.

Our contract recognizes that some issues will take a few days to play out. There's something to the adage, "Let's sleep on it." I'm a night person, so this agreement also lets my husband say "enough for now" without being accused of a capital crime.

We will kiss each other good morning and good night.

We tossed this one in without realizing how rewarding it might be. The great thing about this agreement is

> *"Our marriage is more durable and flexible as a result [of our prenuptial agreement]."*

that it unhooks caring from mood, and connects it instead to commitment.

My husband and I kiss each other at the endpoints of each day, not as a reward for exemplary marital behavior, but because we believe we benefit from consistently expressed affection. Oh, sure, those kisses are awfully perfunctory at times, but they're there, reminding us that we are, too.

We will always give each other another chance.

If my husband and I have learned anything in our lives, it's that we all make mistakes. Instead of assigning blame or punishment, we believe forgiveness is much more healing. I cannot remember ever specifically citing this condition, but I'm convinced its presence in our contract has done a lot to create the safety and security we both crave. Imagine living with the constant promise of another chance. This clause, by the way, does not eliminate how each of us feels about the other forgetting a birthday or not balancing the checkbook. But it does eliminate blame and groveling.

Now into our second year of marriage, we've had an opportunity to put most of these provisions into play. What started out as an evening's project has evolved into a living document that seems to grow right along with us, and I'm convinced our marriage is more durable and flexible as a result.

Public Policy Reforms Would Strengthen Marriage

by Maggie Gallagher

About the author: *Maggie Gallagher is the author of* Enemies of Eros *and* The Abolition of Marriage: How We Destroy Lasting Love, *from which this viewpoint is excerpted.*

The next great American challenge is to get out of the business of merely managing the decline of the family and begin the process of rebuilding it. To re-create marriage, we have to step back from the angry couple and look at marriage in a wider context: What incentives are now in place, and what incentives does marriage require? How can we restore some traditional supports, and how can we come up with innovative ways to nurture marriage? People who wish to marry are attempting to do something—something more than merely living together until they drift apart. How can law, culture, and public policy conspire to help more Americans achieve their heart's desire?

Do not look for or expect easy answers—a single silver bullet to slay the divorce dragon. Piece by piece, the cultural, political, and economic edifice supporting marriage has been taken down, often only half-consciously, by courts and reformers who sincerely believed they were expanding "personal choice." Reconstructing marriage will require taking a serious, unsentimental look at a wide array of public policy decisions in the light of a new understanding of what marriage as an institution requires. . . .

Welfare Policy

Welfare policy has been discussed extensively elsewhere. To that currently raging debate I would only add this proviso: The primary goal of welfare reform should not be to save money, but to reverse the trend toward unwed motherhood. Whether they admit it or not, the Republicans' approach to welfare hinges on curbing the skyrocketing illegitimacy rate. If welfare reform does not succeed in reducing out-of-wedlock births, then scaling back the federal financial commitment will have the Dickensian results its opponents prophesy.

As of this writing, Congress appears poised to pass the Senate's welfare package, avoiding a family cap and a ban on welfare to underage mothers in favor of a five-year time limit on benefits, a requirement that half of welfare recipients work, and the transformation of Aid to Families with Dependent Children (AFDC) from an entitlement to a block grant. [Welfare reform was passed in 1996.]

> *"There is something wrong with a society that can explicitly tell its teenagers not to get married but is afraid to warn them against out-of-wedlock births."*

If the goal is curbing illegitimacy, the Senate approach has serious drawbacks. Workfare [requiring welfare recipients to work] has been tried extensively and found to be both very expensive and only modestly useful in getting women off welfare. Pushing workfare is really part of the continuing and (I believe) futile attempt to remake the single-parent family into a functional substitute for marriage. If most educated divorced women regain their family income only through remarriage, can we really expect poor, uneducated, underparented young women to singlehandedly raise decent kids and pull them out of poverty?

For the purpose of ending a culture of dependency, a five-year time limit may be worse than useless. For the average teenager, much less a poor, inner-city kid, five years seems an eternity. The Senate proposal thus invites a vulnerable young woman to have a baby she cannot support and then cuts her off after she has made decisions (like quitting school or having another baby) that make it virtually impossible for her to become self-supporting. Similarly, while one can imagine asking her to give up for adoption a baby she cannot take care of, one cannot really ask the same woman, five years later, to ditch a preschooler just because she is poor.

Far more important is ending welfare for underage mothers. In 1993, 369,000 babies were born to unmarried teenagers, about 30 percent of all out-of-wedlock births. If we aren't willing to tell these poor, undereducated unmarried girls categorically that they should not be raising children alone, we aren't serious about ending poverty or making a start on rebuilding marriage.

Instead of routinely giving custody of babies to girls too young to drive a car or sign a contract, the law should require that every baby born in America be under the guardianship of a competent adult. That adult will assume full legal and financial responsibility for the child until the minor mother grows up and demonstrates (through marriage or a full-time job) she is capable of providing her children with a home. If the girl's parents (or other friend or relative) are unwilling or unable to provide such a guarantee, the baby should be made available for adoption.

Welfare is not the only issue. Our bumper crop of children having children is in part the fruit of a 1972 federal law that made it illegal for schools receiving federal funds to expel students or restrict their participation in school activities because of pregnancy or parenthood. The law produced its intended result: The high school completion rate of young teen mothers jumped from 19 percent in 1958 to 56 percent in 1986, according to the Alan Guttmacher Institute's 1986 study. At the same time, the proportion of births to unmarried girls skyrocketed. A high school diploma has proved no substitute for marriage, either for babies or for their childishly young mothers. Indeed, even a college degree does not inoculate youngsters from the disadvantages of growing up outside of marriage. The federal government should get out of the business of trying to make unwed motherhood a viable social institution: Using the power of the purse, Washington has done much to elevate unwed motherhood in the minds of youngsters from a moral wrong to a Constitutional right. School districts should once again be permitted to require pregnant girls (and where identifiable, the boys who impregnate them) to attend special schools during the pregnancy. Such a policy recognizes that getting pregnant is not a pathological behavior, but a profoundly attractive human achievement, one that other girls are likely to envy and emulate, particularly in poor neighborhoods where neither marriage nor career appears to be likely possibilities.

At the same time, we should change the emphasis in school classrooms from merely combating teen pregnancy to discouraging out-of-wedlock births. This need not (and ought not) require stigmatizing children from broken homes. Children without fathers know better than anyone else the special strains of life outside of mar-

> *"Married families have been treated by federal policymakers as a kind of cash cow . . . to generate tax revenues."*

riage. But in current health and family life textbooks, marriage is treated as a small footnote in the much larger and more important story of child abuse or of family diversity. Much of the small space devoted to marriage is taken up by dire warnings against that fifties' bugaboo, teenage marriage.

Surely there is something wrong with a society that can explicitly tell its teenagers not to get married but is afraid to warn them against out-of-wedlock births for fear of sounding overly moralistic. We owe our young people a well-grounded knowledge of the economic, social, health, and emotional advantages of a good-enough marriage. All federally funded sex education and family life programs should be required to focus on the value of a good-enough marriage for adults and children.

Welfare Policies Are Self-Defeating

Moreover, transcending the welfare debate's narrow focus on changing the behavior of poor women, we must seek policies to stem the falling wages of men, particularly poor, black inner-city men. We need to reevaluate and reform current job-training programs, including workfare, that are available to or are successful with women only and relax federal regulations to permit local inner-city school districts to experiment with programs aimed specifically at vulnerable inner-city boys, including single-sex public schools.

The next step is to recognize that the whole underlying premise of our welfare system—reserving scarce public dollars for only the poorest, who inevitably turn out to be single mothers—may be self-defeating.

> *"Public policy . . . tax[es] married families at unprecedented rates to provide a wide array of benefits available only to single mothers."*

Norms are not self-sustaining. When government is as big and as powerful as it is in modern-day America, when it consumes so much of individual and national resources, then it inevitably plays a key role (whether we like it or not) in maintaining norms of behavior. When public policy refuses to recognize, reward, and reinforce norms, the norms begin to evaporate. Rearing children is arduous, time-consuming, and expensive. Single people have responded to the new erosion of marital supports by avoiding marriage altogether. Married families have responded by putting more and more family members in the workforce, laboring longer hours, cutting back severely on the number of children they have, and, in the ensuing distress, divorcing more often.

The illegitimacy rate is skyrocketing both because married people have so few children and because single mothers have more. Married couples can stop having children, or single women can start having them. Either way, the illegitimacy rate jumps.

Looking at the troubled state of the African American family, we must recognize that the relative childlessness of stable marriages is almost as serious a problem as the fertility of the unwed—at least insofar as the one- or no-child family represents not the fulfillment but the frustration of the wishes of overworked, overtaxed, divorce-anxious married couples. Married families have been treated by federal policymakers as a kind of cash cow that can be relied on to generate tax revenues for any and all government needs. In economic terms, public policy now systematically discriminates against the married by taxing married families at unprecedented rates to provide a wide array of benefits available only to single mothers or to families of such low incomes that even working-class married couples do not qualify.

A Recent Policy Trend

This pronounced public policy tilt against marriage was not always the case. Until the late sixties, for example, New York City public housing projects gave a preference to low-income married couples. But along with federal money came federal strings: Washington insisted that public housing dismantle this preference for the married poor. The result is not only an erosion in the quality of life at housing projects, but a dismantling of important supports for marriage in the working class. It is a measure of how far marriage has fallen from official favor that the [New York City mayor] Giuliani administration recently braved a controversy to bring back preferences—but only for "working" families, not necessarily for married families. (Meanwhile, in New York City public schools, children are taught that it is a violation of civil rights to "discriminate" on the basis of marital status.) Once again, Washington, D.C., using its immense financial leverage, effectively forbade local communities from supporting marriage.

Working-class families may need some public subsidies. Public housing projects, now obsessed with maintaining racial balance, would be far better off if the federal government permitted them to reserve a substantial portion of their slots for low-income married couples. To offset the marriage penalty working-class couples face, Congress should replace the earned-income tax credit with a "marriage bonus" administered through the tax code for all married families with incomes of less than 50 percent of the average married family.

But all married families need to be allowed to keep more of their own private income for the vital public purpose of rearing children. In recent decades, the economic basis of marriage has been allowed to erode, particularly in tax policy. Federal tax relief has been targeted at taxpayers in general and at low-income families, disproportionately single mothers. Meanwhile, the tax burden has shifted heavily onto married couples with children. To restore the protection that has been lost to inflation, the dependent exemption would have to be more than tripled, from about $2,500 to nearly $8,000 a year.

Married Families Need Not Apply

For low-income families, the recently expanded earned income tax credit helps offset tax increases. But the earned income tax credit, besides being subject to extraordinary rates of fraud, is another example of family policy aimed at incomes so low most married families need not apply. Less than 20 percent make under $25,000 a year, the approximate income cutoff for the earned income tax credit. By contrast, the majority of single moms makes less than $15,000 a year. Policies like the earned income tax credit thus protect most single mothers, but relatively few married couple families. Even the proposed $500 child tax credit . . . was designed to deliver disproportionate benefits to the lower middle class, ignoring the relative disadvantage now built into the tax code for all married couples with children. The question of fairness involved in the child credit or dependent exemption is not whether a couple with three kids making $100,000 should pay more taxes than a similar couple making $40,000. (They should and do.) The question is whether a family of five making $100,000

> *"Policies like the earned income tax credit . . . protect most single mothers, but relatively few married couple families."*

should be asked to pay the same taxes as a bachelor making $100,000 a year.

The theory behind the generous protections for the average family built into the fifties tax code is simple: Among the competing public interests of the nation, the needs of children ought to come first. Families must be allowed to keep all the income they reasonably need to rear children, before making other contributions to the national welfare. By allowing inflation to gut the dependent exemption, we have implicitly transformed children (and the marriages that protect them) from public contributions into private consumption items.

How to Stabilize Marriage

Probably the most straightforward way to stabilize marriage, without discriminating either for or against working mothers, is to restore the value of the dependent exemption to $8,000 per dependent (which happens to be almost exactly the amount the government estimates each child costs a middle-class family in out-of-pocket expenses) and index it to inflation. Such a policy would relieve the economic distress of many married families (who have been increasingly taxed as if they had the discretionary income of childless singles), provide more money for day care for those women who choose to work, aid families in which parents work in shifts in order to care for their own children, and help many other women withdraw from the labor force, perhaps temporarily or part time.

> *"It is the collapse of marriage that has fueled the ever-increasing welfare state."*

Allowing married families to provide for their own needs will be expensive. There are few short-term supply-side returns to family tax cuts, which is why economic conservatives tend to oppose them. Instituting them will require making politically painful choices in the federal budget. The returns come not in next year's revenues but in the long-range increase in productivity and social stability that will take place when a greater proportion of American children grow up under the protection that a good-enough marriage provides. The hidden crime tax, the ignorance tax, the drug tax, and the explicit taxes required to fund an ever-increasing welfare state all take a deep toll on the economy and an even deeper toll on American civilization.

For, above all, it is the collapse of marriage that has fueled the ever-increasing welfare state, and economic conservatives are fooling themselves if they believe they can do more than retard its political momentum in the long run, absent a revival of marriage. American self-reliance has ultimately been based not on rugged individualism but on the mutual interdependence of husband and wife, the donation of the self in the service of children and community. Where after all do the clients of the client-state come from? A decrease in the divorce and illegitimacy rate would cut the ranks of the homeless, the welfare dependent, the drug addicted, and above all the criminal class.

Changes like these are not small or cheap. They will happen only when married families begin to view themselves (as senior citizens do) as a coherent interest group or when society as a whole recognizes the central importance of marriage. Fortunately, there are encouraging signs of the public's willingness to tackle the problems of marriage as an institution. For example, since the late eighties, according to Gallup polls, a majority of Americans once again say that divorce should be made more difficult to obtain. Americans want marriage. By a margin of 76 percent to 19 percent, or four to one, Americans would rather live in a place "that strongly upholds traditional family values" than a place "that is very tolerant of nontraditional lifestyles."

Indissoluble Marriages Would Strengthen Marriage

by Christopher Wolfe

About the author: *Christopher Wolfe is a professor of political science at Marquette University and the president of the American Public Philosophy Institute in Milwaukee, Wisconsin.*

I've probably been hanging around [political science professor and writer] Hadley Arkes too long. Hadley has a way of coming up with wonderful little pieces of proposed legislation whose main point is less the legislation itself than the principle it establishes or absence of sound principle it exposes. For example, he has proposed that legislation prohibiting abortions in the third trimester (after "viability") be introduced in Congress, in order to force pro-choice representatives to make arguments of some kind as to why such legislation should not pass. They surely would oppose it, but what could they give as a reason for doing so? Such a law might not save many lives in the short run— there are relatively few third-trimester abortions ("only" about 17,000 a year)— but it would be valuable because it would reveal more clearly and publicly the true foundations of the pro-choice position: radical autonomy, even to the point of destroying early, developing human life.

A similar kind of proposal has occurred to me. It's not a proposal that is likely to have much of a practical impact. I'm not even sure that it is one we should want to press for. But I think it would be interesting to put forward, in order to reveal more clearly and publicly something that many of us know is true, but that orthodox liberals would deny. This proposal concerns not abortion, but marriage.

Indissoluble Marriage

The proposal is this: let us amend state marriage laws so as to make it *possible* for a man and a woman to choose freely to enter into an indissoluble marriage. Note: possible, not mandatory.

The details of such a law would have to be worked out. Perhaps, to minimize

From Christopher Wolfe, "The Marriage of Your Choice," *First Things*, February 1995. Reprinted by permission.

certain objections, it would have to be restricted to people who are at least twenty-one. Presumably, some grounds for legal declaration of the nullity of the marriage ab initio (annulments) would have to be maintained, though in a form that did not become a gaping loophole. (Admittedly, this might not be a simple task.) Indissolubility is, of course, completely compatible, in principle, with legal separation for cases in which the well-being (physical, financial, and otherwise) of a spouse is threatened by continued living together. But these practical issues aside, it is intriguing to speculate about the debate that might emerge from such a proposal.

No-Fault Divorce

As the current legal order stands, *all* American marriages can be dissolved by divorce decrees. "No-fault" divorce legislation swept the country in the 1960s, and became law in all the states. It was based on the assumptions that (a) marriages involving irreconcilable differences ought not to be maintained compulsorily by the law, and (b) the harms of clogging up the courts with bitter divorce battles outweighed any benefits of requiring that divorce be based on some legally proven "fault" of one of the partners.

It is hard to know the extent to which the increased rate of divorce today is affected by the relative ease of legal divorce. That is, it is difficult to know whether no-fault divorce is a cause or merely a symptom. Of course, no one would contend that no-fault divorce is *the* cause of a high divorce rate; but it would certainly not be unreasonable to suppose that it is a significant contributing factor.

> *"The increased rate of divorce today is affected by the relative ease of legal divorce."*

No-fault divorce legislation was, from one perspective, merely part of a larger cultural change that expanded personal autonomy, not merely in marriage laws, but in the area of sexuality generally (and more broadly as well). It is surely not the sole cause of declining family stability.

On the other hand, even if it is, to a considerable extent, an epiphenomenon of deeper cultural changes, once ensconced in the law, divorce becomes part of the "moral ecology" of our culture and shapes the attitudes and expectations of many citizens about marriage. The free terminability of marriage changes the definition of marriage, just as there is an essential difference between a contract terminable at will by either party and a contract terminable only after ten years. Such laws promote a certain *image* of marriage, with terminability as one of its features.

The Catholic View

Of particular interest is the question of its impact on traditional communities within the nation that have principled commitments to different views of marriage. For example, Catholic parents can raise their children to understand divorce as a "legal fiction." They can tell their children that when they say that so-and-so is "divorced," they don't really mean that his or her marriage bond with the original spouse has been broken—that bond, after all, is unbreakable—but that our particular society (wrongly) regards it as having been broken.

But in the real world of raising children and of growing up in society, it is difficult to maintain this understanding. Children—somewhat understandably, I suppose—get annoyed if, every time they refer to a "divorced" person,

> *"The free terminability of marriage changes the definition of marriage."*

they have to hear mom or dad trot out the homily: "Of course, they're not *really* divorced, because . . ." Nor can they themselves, when they are in normal conversation with their friends—many of whom are non-Catholics or "Americanized" Catholics who don't accept the Church's teaching on marriage—be expected to trot out the homily when there are references to divorce. Moreover, as they associate with more and more friends whose parents are divorced, whose "moms" or "dads" are not "really" their moms or dads, but their real mom's or dad's second spouse—and who may be very nice people, whom their friends regard as their genuine parents—it becomes harder to keep the distinction sharp. And so they end up absorbing from a society where there are frequent, casual references to and experiences of divorce, almost as if by osmosis, views antithetical to what Catholics believe to be the truth about marriage.

The intermediate position between the Catholic view and the secular liberal view is the "privatization" of our moral views: divorce—the fact that the marriage is ended, the bond broken—is subtly assumed to be a reality, but "we Catholics" don't do it. But, deprived of its foundation in "reality," such a view easily degenerates into the view that "no divorce" is a "rule" for Catholics. And once it becomes a "rule," it can easily be challenged as "moral absolutism," "uncompassionate," "rigid," and so on, and something subject to change. It is this process that probably explains why so many modern Catholics have come to accept divorce and remarriage.

The Law Is Not Neutral

I have spelled out this line of reasoning (less a matter of logic perhaps, than what might be called "socially conditioned" thinking) because of the likely liberal response to the proposal that American law permit indissoluble marriage. That response would go something like the following. "It is not true that American law is incompatible with indissoluble marriage. There is absolutely nothing to prevent two people who believe that marriage is indissoluble from getting married and staying married, fixed in their belief that divorce is a fiction. Our law simply declines to *compel* all people to enter indissoluble marriages, since many of us do not believe that marriages are indissoluble. The law is neutral, because it permits everyone to live consistently with his or her own beliefs on the subject."

There is a core of truth in this, of course. There is no reason, for example, why Catholics could not recognize that they live under two laws, a civil law and their own canon law, and treat the civil law on marriage, with its permission of divorce, as irrelevant to them.

My contention, however, is that the law is not neutral. In treating marriage as a contract revocable at the will of either party, the law adopts one of the competing views of marriage. It does not permit people to really *bind* themselves to a permanent and exclusive marriage, by reinforcing the personal commitment with the force of the law.

Yet some people might want to have that unbreakable, legally enforceable bond for themselves, on various grounds. It would provide very strong incentives for each person to make his or her own initial decision to marry carefully and reassure each person about the seriousness with which his or her prospective spouse makes that decision. It would provide similar incentives for each of them to exert the maximum effort to make the marriage work, and, again, reassure each one that his or her spouse has the same incentives. This could be viewed as one "strategy" for maximizing the likelihood of a successful marriage. Liberal divorce law not only rejects this strategy as a general one for all marriages—it rules it out *even for those who would freely choose it. . . .*

Forced to Be Free

The idea of permitting decisions involving lifelong commitments is one that liberals or "autonomists" have a great deal of difficulty—I won't say accepting, but rather—tolerating. Why? Perhaps it would not be unfair to make the following comparison. Welfare state liberals today are often critical of the free market, because those who suffer in it (e.g., the unemployed) are immediately in view, while its advantages (because they are the result of indirect effects, especially in the form of incentives) tend to be seen only in the long run. Similarly, social liberals have a great deal of difficulty accepting restrictions on divorce, because those who suffer from such restrictions are immediately and easily observable, while the benefits of such restrictions (because they flow from indirect effects on incentives) are not as easily identifiable. The common element underlying the two views is misplaced—because it is based on excessively short-term views—compassion.

> *"[Indissoluble marriages] would provide very strong incentives for each person . . . to marry carefully."*

"But the law is neutral in a broader sense," someone might argue. "Its duty is to preserve personal freedom or autonomy, and genuine autonomy requires that a person always have the ability to change his or her mind." Perhaps the liberal apologist would draw a parallel between indissoluble marriage and a voluntarily made contract to enter a state of slavery: just as American law will not recognize a contract to enter into slavery—since it would constitute a giving up of the very freedom the law is intended to protect—so it will not enforce a contract to establish an indissoluble marriage, since that would restrict the freedom of the party to change his or her mind. A legal order protecting true autonomy is inconsistent with laws permitting the giving up of autonomy, even voluntarily.

I was told a story recently by a person who had a conversation with one of the Uniform Law Commissioners influential in the rise and triumph of no-fault divorce laws. The possibility of formulating the law with an "opt-

> *"[Indissoluble marriage] could be viewed as one 'strategy' for maximizing the likelihood of a successful marriage."*

out" provision for those who might prefer *not* having the option of no-fault divorce was raised, and drew the immediate response, "That would be against public policy."

What this makes clear is that liberal society is not neutral on the autonomous life (as "autonomy" is conceived by contemporary liberals). Traditional communities—such as groups of Catholics—within the larger political community that deny the absolute value of the autonomous life are put at a distinct disadvantage, as things stand, by American law. They are not permitted to make legally enforceable contracts binding themselves to abide by what they take to be the moral law. From one perspective, one might say that they are "forced to be free."

Another Argument

Another possible line of opposition to a law that would permit indissoluble marriages is quite different: indissoluble marriages are sometimes wrong, not because they violate the autonomy of the spouses, but because they harm third parties, namely the children of marriages where the partners have come to dislike each other so much that they create a pervasive atmosphere of mutual hostility deleterious to the well-being of the children. According to this line of reasoning, the state has an obligation not to permit indissoluble marriage contracts because of the possible harm to some children, in whom the state has an interest independent of the marriage itself.

But this case must actually be pressed much further than might appear at first glance. Freely chosen indissoluble marriage contracts would not be incompatible with decrees of legal separation. The fact that the marriage bond is held to be unbreakable is not inconsistent with an allowance, where extreme circumstances permit, of legal separation, either to protect the well-being and safety of one of the spouses themselves, or of the children. What it would prohibit, for those who choose indissoluble marriage, is legal remarriage.

The Effect on Children

Therefore the case for protecting third parties would have to be based on the contention that in some cases children would positively benefit from having one of their parents marry a new spouse. But this is a less compelling argument because it moves from something that is "necessary"—removing the children from circumstances that are positively harmful to them—to something that is "beneficial"—that the children be put in circumstances that are "better." But the state cannot be given the power to determine and enforce what is merely "better" for children. After all, if the argument were that the children would be better off with remarriage, that would seem to imply a ground for the state to *command* remarriage—an argument no one is likely to make.

Moreover, it is not difficult to raise serious questions, on the basis of contemporary social science research, about whether in the aggregate—that is, across all of society—children are better off under a regime of easy divorce than under a regime of indissoluble marriage (with legal separation available in extreme circumstances). Studies like Judith Wallerstein and Joan Berlin Kelly's *Surviving the Break-Up*, based on a long-term study of the effects of divorce on children—at the very least (and in spite of the authors' own commitments to the maintenance of divorce laws)—make it impossible to say with any certainty that children are better off in a society where divorce is easily obtainable. It is certainly true that some children suffer greatly under the influence of some bad marriages. But it is no less true that some children suffer terribly in cases of divorce, even of "bad" marriages.

> *"Freely chosen indissoluble marriage contracts would not be incompatible with decrees of legal separation."*

Nor is it possible to measure the suffering occasioned by the additional divorces that occur in a regime that permits divorce, when such marriages might have been saved and made good in a regime that did not permit divorce. Nor—given that children of divorce are distinctly more likely themselves to have marriages ending in divorce—can we measure the extra suffering occasioned for the children involved in those additional divorces.

At the very least, it is not possible for liberals to take a stand on these intensely contestable questions, use that stand to ground a prohibition of indissoluble marriages, and then legitimately claim to be establishing a "neutral" legal framework for society. A law that does not at least *permit* indissoluble marriages cannot maintain a pretense of neutrality.

Hope Versus Belief

It is not only liberals who might oppose a law that permits indissoluble marriages. Those who fully accept the indissolubility of marriage might also do so. Their argument might take the following form. "It is true that marriage is indissoluble and that it is sad that American law does not reflect that truth (although that law may be unavoidable, given that the social mores would not support a law that made all marriages indissoluble). Nonetheless, a legal permission for some indissoluble marriage contracts would make things worse, because it would systematize the dissolubility of marriage more completely. As things stand, all marriages are technically dissoluble, given the availability of no-fault divorce, but the law still treats marriage as a single entity and most ordinary people still enter into marriage with a sense that they are doing so 'until death do us part.' By forcing people to choose between a specifically dissoluble and a specifically indissoluble marriage contract, the law may actually heighten many couples' sense of the dissolubility of their marriages. On the whole, then, such a law would make the situation even worse."

This argument is not without considerable force. It turns, in great measure, on exactly what the sense of most Americans entering marriage today is. Do most Americans consider their *own* marriages as "indissoluble" (irrespective of what laws they might favor)? If so, the case for not forcing people formally to choose between dissoluble and indissoluble marriage contracts is stronger.

But I tend to think that we would be deceiving ourselves if we viewed the current situation in that way. It is, unfortunately, easy to mistake a *hope* that marriage will last forever with a *belief* that it *necessarily* will. There is no evidence in our current society that genuinely indissoluble marriage has widespread support. Under these circumstances—an assessment that reflects a deeper disillusionment with contemporary American mores—worrying about whether the institution of marriage will be weakened by permitting indissoluble marriages seems rather farfetched.

And yet, paradoxically, it is the very strength of the ideal of marriage "till death do us part" that may be one of the most important reasons why this proposal is unlikely to be adopted in American law today.

A Two-Tier System of Marriage

The practical effect of a law permitting indissoluble marriages would be to create a two-tier system of marriages in this country: those that are dissoluble and those that are indissoluble. And such a two-tier system would offend democratic egalitarian sensibilities.

Why, you ask? Don't democracies tend to place a high value on personal liberty, and wouldn't such a law give people more freedom to choose which kind of marriage they want?

The underlying problem for the liberal is that the lover does not seek freedom, but union with the beloved. The lover wants the beloved to give love freely, but the lover may also

> *"What [indissoluble marriages] would prohibit . . . is legal remarriage."*

want to bind himself or herself to the other and to give and receive a permanent and exclusive love. And the signs by which the lover binds himself or herself to the beloved are of enormous importance, especially given the vulnerability of one who gives himself or herself completely to another.

In the real world, how would romantic relationships be affected by the existence of two different kinds of marriage contracts, one dissoluble and the other indissoluble? Let's face it: while many people would opt for the dissoluble contract, because of their uncertainties about the vagaries of married love, many people (most? I doubt it, but who knows?) would regard the indissoluble contract as the expression of a fuller, more complete, more unconditional love. The other kind would be—in a colloquial phrase some kids use—"cheap-lousy."

> *"Children of divorce are distinctly more likely themselves to have marriages ending in divorce."*

It is almost amusing to imagine the dilemma confronted by the young lover trying to decide which form of marriage to propose to his beloved—and especially the tactfulness and imagination with which he would have to present his arguments for proposing marriage with a "bail-out" provision. ("When you get to know me better, you may discover that I am utterly unworthy of you, and far be it for me to lock you into a marriage with someone who will make you unhappy." Presumably the more romantic ones would avoid: "Who knows whether we'll be happy? Let's not take too big a chance.")

The very existence of an indissoluble marriage contract would be, for many, a sign of contradiction: an accusation to those unwilling to make the unconditional commitment, a kind of implied charge of "second-class" love. I doubt that a modern democratic society would permit such a distinction. It would prefer to prohibit the sign of a more unqualified love, in order to prevent the implication that other loves were lesser ones.

As I suggested above, I'm not entirely sure whether this proposal is worth acting on. I *am* convinced it is worth thinking about, and getting other people to think about: the ensuing discussion should make it clear that liberal law is distinctly *not* neutral on this subject; it is distinctly engaged in propagating its own moral views.

Prohibiting Teen Marriage Would Strengthen Marriage

by Edward N. Peters

About the author: *Edward N. Peters directs the Office for Canonical Affairs for the Diocese of San Diego and is a judge on the diocesan and appellate tribunals.*

New annulment petitions are assigned by our judicial vicar to the tribunal judges on the first day of the month. Retrieving mine from the shelf, I know before cracking a file that at least one-fourth of my cases will involve a teen-age petitioner or respondent. In many months that percentage will exceed one-third, and in a significant number of all cases both the petitioner and respondent will have been teen-agers at the time of their wedding. That teen-age marriages are markedly prone to failure is not surprising. That modern canon law still considers a 14-year-old ready for marriage is.

Raising the Minimum Age for Marriage

Until . . . 1917, canon law had basically considered anyone above the age of 12 capable of marriage. Thus, when the 1917 Code of Canon Law raised the minimum age for marriage in the church to 14 for girls and 16 for boys, the change was greeted as an improvement that recognized that something beyond mere reproductive ability was required for Christian marriage.

But the ages established for canonical marriage at the opening of the 20th century are still considered sufficient at its close, despite the fact that numerous insights into Christian marriage have been gained during the ensuing decades, and despite the fact that, in those nations most directly affected by Canon 1083 of the 1983 code, the average age for marriage has climbed well out of the teen-age years into the mid-20's. One might think of it this way: Canon law allows children to marry in the church years before the proprietor of a bowling alley will let them play pinball past 10 P.M. without parental supervision.

The idea of children hardly into their adolescent years being allowed to marry is a little embarrassing, and canonists queried on the topic usually reply that very few 14-year-olds get married anymore. Canon law, we add, was meant to apply in a wide variety of cultures, including those in which 14-year-olds marry happily (just where that land is we leave to anthropologists to determine). In any case, we note that boys cannot marry until they are 16. Obviously, not all questioners are satisfied with these replies.

In the face of continuing criticisms of canonical approbation for teen-age weddings, canonists will next cite Canon 1071 and, with less rubescence, point out that it requires approval of the "local ordinary" for weddings "which cannot be celebrated or recognized in accord with the norm of civil law." Presumably some teen-age weddings fall under this heading. Moreover, when the parents of minors are either unaware

> *"Teen-age marriages are markedly prone to failure."*

of their children's nuptial plans or are reasonably opposed to them, Canon 1071 calls for consultation with the ordinary. But for several reasons, Canon 1071 represents only a narrowing of the channel through which failed teen-age marriages continue to flow.

First, canonical training for pastoral ministers is not what it used to be, and Canon 1071 is sometimes simply overlooked by priests and deacons ignorant of its existence. Second, a surprisingly long list of diocesan personnel qualify as "local ordinaries" for purposes of consultation (Canon 134), a fact that facilitates inconsistent approaches toward teen-age marriages within the same local church, approaches that might not even be those of the diocesan bishop.

Third, beyond the dubious implication that parents' opposition to their children's teen-age wedding plans could be deemed by ministers as *unreasonable*, hence exempting those ministers from any consultation requirement, there is still no *parental* consultation requirement even in cases where parental opposition is considered reasonable. Fourth, 18- and 19-year-olds, still teen-agers and still prone to failed marriages, are not covered by the terms of Canon 1071 because they are not canonically considered "minors" (Canon 97). For all of these reasons, Canon 1071 is not much of a deterrent to teen-age weddings.

Finally, if we church lawyers are particularly hard pressed by challenges to the canons on teen-age weddings, we occasionally point the finger at parishes, since, after all, "pastors are to take care that youths are prevented from celebrating marriages before the age at which marriage is usually celebrated in accord with the accepted practice of the region" (Canon 1072). Such an attitude, of course, does little to cool the feud between tribunal personnel and parochial ministers that simmers in some places.

The Front Lines

Pastors and parish staff are in the front lines of the teen-age wedding crisis; they have to deal with Romeo and Juliet sitting in their offices and demanding a wedding date. By the time we canon lawyers see R & J in the tribunal some years after the divorce, they are claiming, often quite correctly, that their grave lack of discretion at the time of their teen-age wedding is grounds for an annulment under Canon 1095. In brief, we canonists get to deal with older, more mature people who can see their juvenile errors; pastors, meanwhile, remain saddled with star-struck children.

As a practical matter, many factors blunt the effectiveness of Canon 1072 in pastoral life. Among these factors, I think, are Rome's restriction of prohibitory powers over weddings to diocesan bishops (who, in some places, have tried to curb teen-age weddings on their own) and its reservation of invalidating authority over marriage to itself (Canons 1075 and 1077). Such limitations usually leave parish-based ministers, who perform nearly all church weddings, with little practical support in their efforts against juvenile marriages. Certainly there are priests and deacons whose participation in certain teen-age weddings is, even under current canon law, open to serious criticism, but it is only fair to say that most teen-age weddings cannot, under the current discipline, be stopped no matter how serious are the misgivings of the official witness.

The one thing we canon lawyers cannot explain, though, when confronted about the rules for teen-age weddings, is why the National Conference of Catholic Bishops [N.C.C.B.] has not used its authority under Canon 1083 to raise the age for licit marriage in an effort to stem the stream of doomed teen-age marriages. The authority of the episcopal conference to take such action is unquestionable, and it represents a significant improvement in the 1983 code over the discipline of the 1917 code.

> *"Experience and common sense point to the aggravated failure rate among those who marry even in their late teen-age years."*

The change came about thus. During the lengthy canonical reform process following Vatican II, a proposal to raise the minimum ages for Catholic marriage was considered. While some argued that supermature 14- or 16-year-olds might be hurt by raising the canonical ages for valid marriage, many others argued that legions of immature 14- through 19-year-olds were being lulled into thinking that canonical age was an adequate measure of their matrimonial capacity.

Compromise and Pitfalls

In the end, a compromise was struck. Universal law retained 14 and 16 as the ages for valid marriages of girls and boys. But by adding a second provision to what became Canon 1083, Rome authorized episcopal conferences to recognize the concrete circumstances of marriage in their own territories and to raise the ages for licit marriages within a given nation. Although many episcopal conferences (including Canada, Spain, Switzerland, the Philippines, England and Wales, Poland, China, Gambia, Liberia and Sierra Leone) have taken action under Canon 1083, Paragraph 2, to raise the minimum ages for licit marriage, our

N.C.C.B. is not among them. Rather than speculate on why no action has yet been taken on this matter, perhaps our attention would be better focused on what could be done now. Two approaches seem possible.

The first is simply to raise the minimum age for licit marriage in the United States to 18 for both males and fe-

> *"Teen-age weddings are one of the most consistent, and preventable, mistakes made in marriage today."*

males. This would send a clear message that early teen-age weddings are strongly discouraged. It would remove from parochial and diocesan ministers the immediate pastoral burden of having to explain on a case-by-case basis the many pitfalls of teen-age marriages to people who are generally ill-disposed to hear objections in the first place.

Such a matrimonial policy would not conflict with any other provisions in canon law, and, in virtue of Canon 88, its restrictions could be dispensed in individual circumstances (though one would hope that dispensations would be rare). Finally, raising the minimum ages for licit marriage would eventually result in a reduction of tribunal case loads because the delays required by such policy would facilitate the cooling of passions (not necessarily sexual ones) which currently lead to so many rushed teen-age weddings and failed adolescent marriages.

The second approach is perhaps more challenging, but it offers, I think, greater potential benefit: Raise the licit age for marriage in the United States to 19 or even 20. Eighteen, 19-, even 20-year-olds, especially when they attempt marriage with those the same age, usually do not possess the maturing experience of life that parents, certainly, want to see in their children before marrying. Without necessarily challenging the canonical capacity of such persons to marry, experience and common sense point to the aggravated failure rate among those who marry even in their late teen-age years, and suggest the appropriateness of refusing to permit such weddings, at least without a well-considered dispensation.

Assuming Burdens

There are some obstacles to a supra-majority age restriction on marriage, and these deserve consideration. For example, Canons 97 and 98 combine to declare that those aged 18 and above enjoy the full use of their canonical rights, including, presumably, the right to marry. But is this obstacle to a supra-majority age for licit marriage as compelling as one might at first think? More specifically, might canon law offer any other examples of post-majority age restrictions, including some in specifically sacramental and vocational contexts? The answer is yes.

The transitional diaconate, for example, may not be conferred until age 23, and presbyteral ordination is delayed until age 25 (Canon 1031). Both of these ages are well past civil and canonical majority and are required as a precaution against the immature assuming burdens they are not yet able to handle. Turning to consecrated life—although temporary profession could be made at age 18 (at the very earliest), permanent profession cannot be undertaken until at least age 21 (Canons 656 and 658). Considering that there is no such thing as "temporary marriage," the higher age requirement in religious life seems more relevant to our discussion of marriage.

Natural Rights and Teaching Moments

It might be argued that, while there is a natural right to marry, there is no natural right to ordination or to religious profession, and to the degree that this is true, this might permit ordination and profession age requirements to be higher than those that can be imposed for marriage. But in many other ways, the natural right to marriage has been curtailed by various ecclesiastical regulations. Generally these restrictions on marriage have been imposed with the intention of protecting people from making serious mistakes in entering marriage. And surely teen-age weddings are one of the most consistent, and preventable, mistakes made in marriage today.

> *"Serious consideration should be given to raising the minimum age for licit canonical marriage in the United States to 20 for both men and women."*

The prohibition against mixed marriage found in Canon 1124 is one such example of a restriction on the right to marry. Under pain of illicity, Catholics are forbidden to marry baptized non-Catholics without express permission. True, such dispensations are commonly granted, but there is still a value to requiring those considering interdenominational weddings to explore seriously the implications of such marriages. The requirement of special permission itself serves a teaching function and the process of dispensation provides a structured teaching moment for those considering such an important step.

As a tribunal judge, I see far more cases of marital failure linked to age-based immaturity at the time of contract than I see cases of divorce based on denominational differences at the time of the wedding. To the degree that other tribunal judges and pastoral ministers share that observation—and I think most do—considerable support for raising the licit age for marriage in the United States at least to 18 seems at hand. I personally think that serious consideration should be given to raising the minimum age for licit canonical marriage in the United States to 20 for both men and women. In the meantime, the immediate good that can be accomplished even by raising it to 18 for both sexes seems sufficient to warrant such action being taken by the N.C.C.B. at the earliest possible opportunity.

Counseling Can Strengthen Marriage

by Michael J. McManus

About the author: *Michael J. McManus, a nationally syndicated columnist on ethics and religion, is the author of* Marriage Savers.

A phenomenally successful movement of "marriage-saving" programs is springing up across the continent, and I know firsthand the difference they can make.

Twenty years ago, a project I was working on required me to commute weekly from Connecticut to Washington, D.C. I would board the train at 2 a.m. on Mondays and try to sleep my way down the tracks. After working all week in Washington, I'd arrive home late Friday night. My wife, Harriet, graciously put up with this for months, and even had candle-lit dinners waiting for me at 11 p.m. each Friday.

About this time, some couples at church encouraged us to "go on Marriage Encounter." My first reaction was defensive: "I've got a good marriage, thanks." "No," they insisted, "this is a way to make a good marriage better." To this re- porter, that sounded like a public-relations line, but I kept hearing rave reviews from otherwise sensible people. So I asked Harriet if she wanted to go.

"NO!" she snapped.

"Why not? We've been apart for months. This will be good for us."

"We can't afford it," she answered. Later, the friendly couples prompting me told us our way was already paid.

"By who?" I asked.

"By people who love you."

That impressed me, since we had only been in this church a year or so.

Falling in Love Again

With no more excuses, we set off for the site 70 miles away. Our first surprise was that the couples who had urged us to go had arrived early and fixed a won- derful dinner. That was followed by a series of talks by the lead couples. After

From Michael J. McManus, "The Marriage-Saving Movement," *American Enterprise*, May/June 1996. Reprinted by permission from the *American Enterprise*, a Washington, D.C.-based magazine of politics, business, and culture.

each one, they had attendees write for 10 minutes on a given question. We then met privately with our spouse for 10 minutes to discuss what each had written. The first question was easy: "What is it that I admire about you and about our marriage, and how does it make me feel?" I wrote pages about how wonderful Harriet and our marriage were. When we exchanged notebooks back in our motel room, I noticed Harriet was much less enthusiastic.

> *"Churches and synagogues . . . have an obligation to help couples . . . avoid a bad marriage before it begins."*

Later, the assigned topic was, "What is it that I have not told you that I should have shared?" Harriet wrote this: "When you went to Washington, you abandoned me. You love your work more than me." I felt like I had been punched in the stomach, and asked her to tell me more. "Well, you are not a husband and are not a father! You are never home, except weekends. And even then you are always working. I asked you to take the kids for a 15-minute swim, and you said, 'I don't have time. I have to work.'"

I was so caught up in the difficulty of my work that I had not realized the effect it was having on Harriet. I wept and held her and said, "I don't love my work more than you. In fact, I've hated much of it, because I was failing. Please forgive me."

We fell back in love that weekend. It was like being on a second honeymoon—only better, because we had shared ten years together and rediscovered how much we loved one another. More importantly, my wife and I learned the absolute necessity of setting aside time on a daily basis to listen to one another, read Scripture and pray together. When our kids were young, we'd get up at 6:15 to do it; now it's a more rational hour. No longer does Harriet bottle up her feelings as she once did. And I have become a much better listener.

Marriage Encounter

The central idea behind Marriage Encounter and the other marriage-saving programs is simple. Every church has a marriage-saving resource in its pews—couples who have built rewarding, lifelong marriages. They can help other couples do the same. But they have never been asked, equipped, or inspired to do so. With one exception: For 20 to 25 years, the celibate priests at many Catholic churches have turned marriage preparation over to older couples with solid marriages.

Marriage Encounter is a lay-led movement that originally came out of Catholicism and now involves a dozen denominations. About 2 million couples have attended one of its weekend retreats led by three couples with fulfilling marriages. Studies show that 80 to 90 percent of those attending literally fall back in love.

In Quebec, some Marriage Encounter leaders noticed that a few couples who attended the weekends still ended up getting divorced. Asked why, some of them said, "You were talking about powder-puff problems like poor communication. Our problems were much more serious—like ten years of adultery, an issue that no one mentioned at Marriage Encounter."

In response, Quebec Marriage Encounter couples created a more intensive weekend retreat called *Retrouvaille* (French for "rediscovery," pronounced *retro-vye*) to save marriages headed for divorce. They asked back-from-the-brink couples who had rebuilt marriages after adultery, alcoholism, or abuse to lead the weekends. These veteran survivors speak openly about how they have overcome their problems, and serve as mentors to attending couples. The technique of writing 10 minutes and then talking in private about what each has written is the same as in Marriage Encounter.

Retrouvaille has swept across the border and is now in 100 metro areas in the United States. Its results are spectacular. In Northern Virginia, for example, a fifth of the 400 couples who attended were already separated, yet 79 percent have since managed to rebuild their marriages. In Michigan, where a third of the participants had already filed divorce papers, four-fifths of the unions have been healed. All told, *Retrouvaille* has saved the marriages of 80 percent of the nearly 50,000 Canadian and American couples who have visited a session on the road to divorce.

Local Programs

There are also many local programs that have saved unions headed for divorce court. Jacksonville, Florida's Marriage Ministry is one such. It began when Rev. Dick McGinnis of St. David's Episcopal Church told his congregation one Sunday, "I would like to meet with any couples whose marriages were once on the rocks, but are now in a state of healing. Meet me in the chapel after the service."

He did not know if any couples would come forward, but 10 couples did so, out of a congregation of 180 people. Thrilled, he told them, "I am overwhelmed trying to counsel all the tough marriages in this church. I went to the Lord in prayer, and what came to me was the way Alcoholics Anonymous works: Someone who has successfully overcome the addiction tells how he did it. We need similar couples who can tell how they turned around a bad marriage."

Of the 10 couples, seven agreed to work with him. Their stories were diverse. One woman had been in an adulterous affair for eight years. One man was a bisexual who once had homosexual affairs on the side. Another man was an ex-drunk. The group developed 17 Marriage Ministry action steps—analogous to A.A.'s 12 Steps—on how to save a bad marriage. These 17 "M&M" steps are potentially more far-reaching than A.A.'s 12 Steps, however, because while only a small

> *"Couples approaching marriage desperately need an objective view of their strengths and weaknesses as a pair."*

fraction of Americans are alcoholics, more than half of all marriages are failing.

One of these founding couples illustrated how change could come. The wife explained that her husband was an alcoholic who was out of work for two years. "He would not discipline the children. He threw his clothes all around. All he did in this marriage was foot-ball and the garbage." But then she realized that part of the problem was her "sharp tongue." So she prayed to God to send angels down "to hold my tongue." He noticed right away that she was no longer griping. So he picked up his clothes one day. She was more amorous that night. He thought that was great. She could not change him, but she could change herself, and as she did so, she inspired change on his part.

> *"Those who break their engagements are avoiding a bad marriage before it begins."*

Rev. McGinnis's seven original couples have now worked with 40 troubled marriages in their church, and helped to save 38 of them. That's a 95 percent success rate.

Premarital Inventories

"A dating relationship is designed to conceal information, not reveal it," writes James Dobson in *Love for a Lifetime*. "Each partner puts his or her best foot forward, hiding embarrassing facts, habits, flaws, and temperaments. Consequently . . . the stage is then set for arguments and hurt feelings (after the wedding) that never occurred during the courtship experience."

Given the intrinsic deceptiveness of romance, churches and synagogues (who conduct three-quarters of all first marriages) have an obligation to help couples accomplish two great goals: First, avoid a bad marriage before it begins. Second, learn to resolve the conflicts that are inevitable.

Couples approaching marriage desperately need an objective view of their strengths and weaknesses as a pair. There is no better way to do this than by asking engaged couples to take what is called a "premarital inventory." One of the best is called PREPARE, developed by Dr. David Olson, a family psychologist at the University of Minnesota. It presents 125 statements that both the man and woman are asked to agree or disagree with on separate questionnaires. Many of the items cleverly ask about one's partner—a subject about which people are more honest than they are about themselves:

- Sometimes I am concerned about my partner's temper.
- When we are having a problem, my partner often gives me the silent treatment.
- Sometimes I wish my partner were more careful in spending money.

The inventory is mailed to PREPARE/ENRICH, Inc. with a check for $25, and the easy-to-read results are mailed back to one of 30,000 pastors or counselors who have attended a six-hour training session. More than 1 million couples have taken PREPARE, and half as many have taken its sister inventory,

ENRICH, which measures satisfaction among the already-married.

Remarkably, PREPARE predicts with 86 percent accuracy which couples will divorce, and with 80 percent accuracy who will have a good marriage. More importantly, 10 to 15 percent of those who take the test break off their engagements. Several studies show that these persons' scores are the same as those who marry but later divorce. Thus, those who break their engagements are avoiding a bad marriage before it begins. Others are helped to build a more successful marriage because they are helped to talk through issues while the relationship is young and they are still deeply in love and willing to change for their beloved.

Another major value of PREPARE is that it is simple enough for a mentoring couple to administer. PREPARE/ENRICH provides a kit that a pastor can use to train solidly married couples to undertake marriage preparation with the engaged. One part of the training involves having the potential mentor couple take ENRICH. This has a double value. It gives the mentors a sense of what it is like to take PREPARE, and it helps the pastor be sure a couple has a strong marriage before asking them to serve. Our church has trained 33 mentor couples to meet privately with each engaged couple four times before the wedding and once in the first year of marriage.

> *"[Couples who undergo counseling] are helped to build a more successful marriage."*

My wife, who runs our church's premarital program and now accompanies me in speaking around the country about our marriage-saving work, tells pastors: "A mentor couple can do a better job than a pastor. First, both sexes are involved. I usually understand the woman's concerns, and Mike, the young man's. We can be vulnerable and admit where we made mistakes, which is inappropriate for a pastor. And this is the most rewarding ministry we have ever been involved in. You can do it in the comfort of your own home, as a couple. It has strengthened our own relationship. We have rediscovered what Jesus meant when he said, 'Give, and you shall receive.'"

Predictive, Not Determinative

Three months ago, a black physician in her 30s called to say she and her male friend were considering marriage but were concerned about communication problems they were having. They agreed to come to our marriage prep classes.

My heart sank when I looked at their inventory. They scored 0 on communication and 20 percent on conflict resolution. *Both* said their partner was giving them the silent treatment. Andrew said Gloria made comments that put him down. She wished he were more willing to share his feelings with her. Andrew, an engineer, said, "Gloria doesn't understand how I feel."

"Andrew," I asked, "if you don't share your feelings with Gloria, how can you expect her to understand you? If she calls you at the end of the day, and asks,

'How was your day?' what do you say in response?"

"Great or terrible," he replied.

"Bad answer. What she wants is detail. Even though you are an engineer, you can push yourself to say, 'I had a great day because I finished my project much earlier than expected, and my boss complimented me.' Or, 'It was terrible. I lost two days of work on my computer by pushing the wrong button.' What she wants is detail." Both Harriet and Gloria nodded in agreement.

Three weeks later, they came to our home for another session with big smiles on their faces. I asked, "How is it going? Gloria, is he sharing his feelings with you?"

"He really is," she replied.

"Andrew, do you now feel understood?"

"Yes, and she's not nagging any more."

"How about the silent treatment?" Harriet asked.

"We don't do that any more."

As this story illustrates, the inventory is only *predictive*—not *determinative*. A couple who want to solve their problems can do so. Harriet and I simply used the test to conduct a kind of X-ray of their relationship, and then applied common sense to suggest where Gloria and Andrew could improve their communication. They both had more degrees than Harriet or I, but they lacked our 30 years of experience as a married couple. And their inner-city African-American church had not trained any mentor couples. So they were willing to cross over the cultural barrier and drive 12 miles to our home.

At present, about 250,000 to 300,000 of the 2.4 million couples who marry every year take a premarital inventory, but not 1 percent of churches have trained mentor couples to do this work. Yet it is easy to do so, requiring only the same six-hour seminar attended by clergy. The inventory is a bridge upon which an older generation can meet a younger one and pass on its wisdom. . . .

Proven programs for engaged and married couples exist. They can achieve outstanding results in attacking our nation's number-one problem—break-up of the family. I con-

> *"Proven programs for engaged and married couples exist."*

clude from my work that any church can push its divorce rate below 10 percent, if it so chooses. In the future, no marriage-sponsoring institution has any excuse for not joining the marriage-saving crusade.

Fighting Strengthens Marriage

by Mary Lynn Hendrickson

About the author: *Mary Lynn Hendrickson is the contributing editor of* Salt of the Earth *magazine.*

I'll just come right out and say it: a good fight is an essential ingredient to building a good marriage. I say it in large part because I need to hear it for myself. Like countless other married people—particularly married people who remain active in their church—marital fighting remains a taboo subject. Like confiding that one is a shopaholic or hasn't darkened the door of a confessional in years, admitting to other married people that you and your spouse spar on a fairly regular basis takes on an embarrassed and confidential tone.

Why is that? Such silence, it seems to me, conspires to put modern-day marriages at great risk. To do my part to help dispel this conspiracy of silence, I've made it a personal crusade to break the ice of unacceptability in casual conversation. I like to throw into conversations the fact that my husband and I fight—and I especially like to do it in the company of folks who, like me, are relatively new to marriage. I did just that several months ago, at the conclusion of a work-related conference, when I went out to lunch with an editor I'd just met. She and her husband had been married for only six months. "Really?" said the woman, not once but several times. "You fight about that, too? What a relief!"

Fighting Is Inevitable

Maybe I use the word *essential* to describe a good fight because, in my experience, much fighting seems to be *inevitable*. A quick look at why my husband and I fight might serve to establish that same inevitability for other couples:

• *We fight because of the frayed nerves, shortage of time, and dashed expectations that so frequently accompany modern life.* The fact of the matter is—despite a modest lifestyle and as yet no children—my husband and I find we must punch a time clock each day. And so, in the daily struggle to survive office politics and safeguard job security, like all kinds of people we put our best face for-

From Mary Lynn Hendrickson, "Couples Should Fight for a Good Marriage," *U.S. Catholic*, April 1994. Reprinted with permission from *U.S. Catholic*, published by Claretian Publications, 205 W. Monroe St., Chicago, IL 60606.

ward when working 9 to 5. That means—you guessed it—one of us often gets the brunt of the other's whole day's worth of pent-up frustration.

• *We fight because of gender differences.* Here's just one example of how the fundamental differences in maleness and femaleness have sparked our own personal battle of the sexes. My husband has a very low tolerance for negative remarks and negative thinking in the morning, a phenomenon I used to chalk up to mere differences of personality. I do my spartan best to contribute to a more positive morning-time routine.

But I often slip up: a run in my last pair of navy-blue stockings will do that to me on a morning when I'm al-

> *"A good fight is an essential ingredient to building a good marriage."*

ready running late—and, for me, a quick session of griping and grumbling does wonders to get my attitude back on track. Such was the situation one cold winter morning when our hot water abruptly went out while I was standing in the shower with a head full of shampoo. My husband, standing at the sink shaving, shot back a snarled response. I'm sure I snarled back. Later, as we commuted to work and tempers had subsided, I queried my husband. Hadn't I the right to express myself freely in my own home, particularly in such adverse conditions? Hadn't I the right to be upset with the continuing ineptness of our landlord?

My husband said something, then, that was very enlightening and surprising to me: he said he felt responsible, felt that somehow I was insinuating that I expected him to fix the problem. Responsible? But why? How? What could be the logical reason behind my husband's "feeling responsible"? Well, there wasn't one—only an illogical, irrational one. But it was one, make no mistake, that was culturally inherited and deeply rooted and in the machismo/chivalry remnants of his 20th-century-male psyche. John's explanation solved a whole host of mysteries for me: why it is that so many men go ballistic when, during an argument, a woman bursts into tears; why, during recent negotiations to buy our first home, my husband felt much more of the burden than financially should be the case.

Fights Over Gender Roles

• *We fight because of the erosion of gender-role expectations.* John and I pride ourselves on having a very liberated, modern marriage—one that strives to be free of outmoded cultural assumptions about the supposedly predestined roles of women and men. The problem is: along with all that's stifling, traditional gender roles come with some pretty handy predetermined job descriptions. I thank my lucky stars that I wasn't born 25 years earlier—cooking is far, far down on my list of how I prefer to spend my time. Lucky for me, John enjoys cooking. Lucky for us both that I feel obligated to do my fair share of shoveling snow.

And yet we each have our bad days—days when John feels resentful about initiating dinner and shoveling the sidewalk leaves me running late for work.

Without those handy ol' gender-role job descriptions, we often find ourselves negotiating and renegotiating unpopular household chores on a case-by-case basis. My mom and dad, on the other hand, never had to fight over whose turn it was to make dinner.

• *We fight when we do things together that we've never done before.* I include on this list not only those activities that have been totally new to us both—such as buying a house and, shortly thereafter, having to replace the refrigerator that died—but those familiar activities that we just hadn't *done together* yet: camping together for the first time, disciplining a new puppy, making major do-it-yourself home repairs.

Our first night of camping was indicative: I was used to a leisurely pace in setting up camp, to roughing it, and to relaxing to the quiet sounds of nature. John, on the other hand, was motivated by the importance of hurrying to set up camp and testing out all the new gear we'd gotten as wedding presents. Mutual frustration now operative, I made some snide remark about the irony of hauling out a tape player in the quiet wilds of northern Wisconsin; John calmly explained that he was on vacation, too, and that listening to soft music was *his* way of relaxing.

An Invaluable Tool

But beyond the inevitability of getting into fights, is there something helpful about fighting—in and of itself?

Maybe my husband and I are only kidding ourselves. Maybe we're too accustomed to the rough-and-tumble existence of competing egos that comes from each of us having been raised in large, boisterous families. Maybe we wrongly fall back on our large families as the excuse for our fighting. Nonetheless, I say, a good fight is an invaluable tool for every intimate relationship—marriages included.

Now, by a *good* fight I don't necessarily mean a pull-out-all-the-stops dish-crashing fight. But I do mean a *fight*—not the total calm and control of the euphemistic "disagreement" but something that can resemble an emotional tornado.

What I also mean by a *good fight* is ideally a *fair fight*: no silent treatment, no ultimatums, no stockpiling of old grievances as ammunition for new fights, no "low blows" that come from being mean about issues your partner is embarrassed about—and never, never, ever any emotional or physical battering.

Like most people, I'm far from perfect when it comes to fighting fair. It's the nature of the beast: an outpouring of ugly thoughts and accusa-

> *"A good fight every now and then strengthens the bonds of intimacy."*

tions can quickly cloud my intentions of being fair. But the beauty of fighting is that it requires at least two people, and finger-pointing is the fundamental mode of communication. It's my partner who helps to keep me fair by pointing out whenever I'm being unfair. And so it's by fighting that one learns to fight fair; one needs the hands-on experience.

My own experience tells me that a good fight every now and then strengthens the bonds of intimacy with someone I love. Daring to initiate or perpetuate a fight with a loved one is a real barometer of just how much I trust the relationship. As someone engaged in a Christian marriage, do I really trust my dearest belief that there's unconditional love here? Do I really trust that there can be forgiveness here? Do I truly believe in the power and paradox of redemptive suffering—not only that something good can come of something bad, and that the triumph of that good is all the more triumphant for having come from something so painful? Maybe this is why the church chose to get into the marriage business early on; I, for one, can't imagine a successful marriage without the fundamental Christian principles of unconditional love, forgiveness, and redemptive suffering.

> *"A marriage is a sham unless two people can be totally honest about what hurts and delights them."*

That's why I shake my head whenever I hear a sermon espousing that anger is one of the seven deadly sins. Yet one can ask: is anger really a productive means of problem solving? Don't people often hold back on their hopes and fears *because of* the possibility of an angry response? Maybe it's not conflict they're frightened of but the specter of an explosive reaction.

Marriage Requires Honesty

Perhaps the more helpful path to a loving marriage is learning and exercising self-control. I certainly know my spouse and I struggle with that doubt sometimes. Is it really so horrible that people mask many conflicts they encounter in the 9-to-5 world? Most of us would never think of blowing up at a co-worker who makes a sarcastic remark—so why do we jump all over a spouse who does the same? Shouldn't I treat my husband with the same civility as I do a co-worker, a grocery clerk, a mail carrier, or a bus driver?

But I say no, a marriage is a sham unless two people can be totally honest about what hurts and delights them. And that means being emotionally honest, not just verbally honest. It means offering your total, far-from-perfect self to the full partnership of marriage. It means letting down your guard, letting go of all those useful facades that help people navigate their way through an indifferent world. It means being totally, utterly yourself. The need and the willingness to fight isn't all that different from what Saint Iranaeus said: "The glory of God is the glory of people fully alive."

I don't advocate fighting as a way of testing the strength of a marriage. But neither do I believe that keeping silent or sidestepping conflict in an effort to keep the peace is any way to go about building a marriage—not if your expectations of marriage are the same as mine.

Chapter 1

What do I expect of marriage? Two things: building a bedrock of utmost trust with another human being and, knowing that that bedrock is in place as a sort of psychological safety net, taking those small everyday risks that contribute to my growth as a human being.

Good Practice

But beyond personal growth, fighting, done fairly, gets at one of the important reasons marriage is seen as a sacrament of the Catholic Church. Sacraments exist for us as signs of God's grace and guidance; they are markers that teach us how to successfully live the Christian life with each other. The fighting that goes on in a healthy marriage gives spouses good insight into their relationships with other people, too.

It's in fighting with someone we ultimately love and respect that we learn to take certain emotional risks with others: confronting someone else's negative behavior instead of "swallowing" it and then gossiping about it; having the fortitude to admit when you're wrong; being truly satisfied with "agreeing to disagree."

Case in point: one night I came home from work and told my husband about a major altercation I'd had that day with a co-worker. I was relieved that I seemed to handle it well—not backing down, not being a jerk about it, being able to negotiate some good alternatives. John's eyes lit up. "See," he said. "Aren't you glad I pick fights with you? It's good practice!"

Chapter 2

Is Divorce Harmful?

 CURRENT CONTROVERSIES

Chapter Preface

Since 1975, more than one million children each year have seen their parents divorce—a number that sharply contrasts with the 480,000 children affected by marital breakup in 1960. Although the number of divorcing couples began to decrease after 1980, many social scientists and family therapists have become increasingly concerned about the potentially harmful effects of divorce on such large numbers of children.

Many researchers, such as Barbara Dafoe Whitehead, a former research associate at the Institute for American Values, maintain that children of divorce often suffer long-term damage. According to the information Whitehead gathered from several recent studies on children and divorce, one-third of the surveyed children suffered from depression, emotional insecurity, and school underachievement more than five years after their parents' divorce. In addition, she asserts, children of divorce are more likely to drop out of school, commit crimes, abuse drugs, suffer from physical or sexual abuse, become pregnant as teenagers, or experience serious problems in adult relationships. Because such large numbers of children see their parents divorce, Whitehead concludes, America's societal foundations are threatened by these adverse consequences of marital breakup.

Several researchers dispute Whitehead's conclusions, however. Divorce researcher E. Mavis Hetherington notes that, on average, 20 to 25 percent of children from divorced families experience behavior problems—"about twice as many as the ten percent from nondivorced families. . . . You can say 'Wow, that's terrible,' but it means that 75 to 80 percent of kids from divorced families *aren't* having problems, that the vast majority are doing well." Moreover, John Gottman, a University of Washington psychology professor, argues that concerned parents who carefully plan their divorce and custody arrangements can make their breakup easier on their children. In Gottman's opinion, this option is better than "forcing [children] to live in the donnybrook of their parents' terrible marriage."

Psychologists and social scientists who study divorce have come to no single conclusion about the effects of divorce on children and on society. The authors in the following chapter explore the issues surrounding this controversy.

Divorce Harms Society

by Council on Families in America

About the author: *The Council on Families in America is part of the Institute for Family Values, a public policy research institute in New York City that studies family life and family-related issues.*

America's divorce revolution has failed. The evidence of failure is overwhelming. The divorce revolution—by which we mean the steady displacement of a marriage culture by a culture of divorce and unwed parenthood—has created terrible hardships for children. It has generated poverty within families. It has burdened us with unsupportable social costs. It has failed to deliver on its promise of greater adult happiness and better relationships between men and women.

Relationships between men and women are not getting better; by many measures, they are getting worse. They are becoming more difficult, fragile, and unhappy. Too many women are experiencing chronic economic insecurity. Too many men are isolated and estranged from their children. Too many people are lonely and unconnected. Too many children are angry, sad and neglected.

We believe it is time to change course. The promises of the divorce revolution proved empty, its consequences devastating for both adults and children. It is time to shift the focus of national attention from divorce to marriage. It is time to rebuild a family culture based on enduring marital relationships.

The truth is that every child needs and deserves the love and provisions of a mother and a father. The loving two-married-parent family is the best environment for children—the place where children gain the identity, discipline, and moral education that are essential for their full individual development. And, as the institution which most effectively teaches the civic virtues of honesty, loyalty, trust, self-sacrifice, personal responsibility, and respect for others, the family is an irreplaceable foundation for long-term social efficacy and responsibility.

Marriage Is Under Assault

Marriage is under assault in our society. It is an institution in decline and even disrepute. The eminent demographer Kingsley Davis has said, "at no time in

Excerpted from *Marriage in America: A Report to the Nation* by the Council on Families in America, March 1995. Reprinted by permission of the Institute for Family Values.

history, with the possible exception of Imperial Rome, has the institution of marriage been more problematic than it is today." With each passing year, an ever smaller percentage of the nation's citizens are married and an ever larger percentage of the nation's children live in households that do not consist of two married parents. This steady break-up of the married, mother-father childbearing unit is the principal cause of declining child well-being in our society.

> *"[The divorce revolution] has burdened us with unsupportable social costs."*

Moreover, with each passing year, more and more American children are growing up with little or no direct experience of married life. Many are growing up with little or no confidence that they could be, or even want to be, in a satisfying, enduring marital relationship. Increasingly, the cultural messages the children receive are either indifferent or hostile to marriage. Indeed, it does not seem at all far-fetched to say that we as a society are simply failing to teach the next generation about the meaning, purposes and responsibilities of marriage. If this trend continues, it will constitute nothing less than an act of cultural suicide.

For the average American, the probability that a marriage taking place today will end in divorce or permanent separation is calculated to be a staggering 60%. Again, children are heavily affected. Slightly more than half of divorcing couples in 1988 had children under the age of 18. The odds that a child today will witness the divorce of his or her parents are twice as great as a generation ago. Today, about half of all children in the United States are likely to experience a parental divorce before they leave home.

What's more, a sizable percentage of children who now go through one divorce can expect to go through a second and even third divorce, as many of their parents' remarriages also end in divorce. Quite simply, having children is no longer a strong deterrent to divorce.

A Rise in Marital Unhappiness

Moreover, apart from the trends of divorce and nonmarriage, a growing body of evidence suggests that the quality of married life in America has also taken a turn for the worse. Here is one reason why: in a high-divorce society, not only are more unhappy marriages likely to end in divorce, but in addition, more marriages are likely to become unhappy. For in a society where divorce has become a common and even normative experience, people quite reasonably tend to hedge their bets regarding the durability and even desirability of marriage. We become less willing to invest ourselves fully— our time, resources, dreams, and ultimate commitments—in the institution of marriage. One result is a measurable rise in marital unhappiness.

Our culture has become increasingly skeptical of marriage and of other institutions as well that are thought to restrict or confine adult behavior. In their place, we now put a much higher value on individualism, choice, and unrestricted personal liberty.

As a result, marriage has been losing its social purpose. Instead of serving as our primary institutional expression of commitment and obligation to others, especially children, marriage has increasingly been reduced to a vehicle—and a fragile vehicle at that—for the emotional fulfillment of adult partners. "Till death us do part" has been replaced by "as long as I am happy." Marriage is now less an institution that one belongs to and more an idea that we insist on bending to our own, quite individualistic purposes.

Emotional fulfillment is an important and worthy goal. But it should not be the sole purpose of marriage when children are involved. If marriage is to remain a viable social institution, the self-fulfillment of parents as individuals cannot take precedence over their obligations to children.

A Divorce Culture

In the recent past, divorce was limited to those marriages which had irreparably broken down, often because one spouse was seriously pathological or incompetent. Today, divorce may occur simply because one partner is unhappy or because a better partner has been located. And given the high rate of divorce, more and more possible partners are continually entering the market. Family court judges often seem more interested in promoting "divorce counseling" than in promoting marriage counseling.

The trend toward a divorce culture is also clearly evident in academic research and writing. Much of the scholarly discourse on family issues conducted over the past three decades has contained a strong anti-marriage bias. Many textbooks written for use in schools and colleges openly propagandize against any privileged cultural status for marriage and quite often even against marriage itself.

> *"This steady break-up of the married, mother-father childbearing unit is the principal cause of declining child well-being in our society."*

We are deeply disturbed by this new culture of divorce. While we certainly recognize that, in individual cases, divorce can sometimes be the least bad solution for a highly troubled marriage, our nation's increasingly casual acceptance of divorce as a normative experience for millions of parents and children should be a cause for profound alarm, not resignation and excuse-making.

Divorce Harms Children

by Karl Zinsmeister

About the author: *Karl Zinsmeister is editor in chief of the* American Enterprise, *a conservative journal of opinion.*

Originally, notes family historian John Sommerville, marriage arose to create "security for the children to be expected from the union." Yet nowadays "the child's interest in the permanence of marriage is almost ignored." During the divorce boom that began in the mid-1960s, divorces affecting children went up even faster than divorces generally, and today *most* crack-ups involve kids. Since 1972, more than a million youngsters have been involved in a divorce *each year*.

The result is that at some time before reaching adulthood, around half of today's children will go through a marital rupture. Most of these youngsters will live in a single-parent home for at least five years. A small majority of those who experience a divorce eventually end up in a step-family, but well over a third of them will endure the extra trauma of seeing that second marriage break up.

The typical divorce brings what researcher Frank Furstenberg describes as "either a complete cessation of contact between the non-residential parent and child, or a relationship that is tantamount to a ritual form of parenthood." In nine cases out of ten the custodial parent is the mother, and fully half of all divorce-children living with their mom have had no contact with their father for at least a full year. Only one child in 10 sees his non-custodial parent as often as once a week. Overall, only about one youngster in five is able to maintain a close relationship with both parents.

Joint child custody receives a lot of publicity (it is now allowed in about half the states), but it remains unusual. In California, where it is much more common than anywhere else, only 18 percent of divorced couples have joint physical custody. Most divorced children still live solely with their mothers.

"For most men," sociologist Andrew Cherlin notes, "children and marriage are part of a package deal. Their ties to their children depend on their ties to their wives." Studies show that remarriage makes fathers particularly likely to reduce involvement with the children from their previous marriage.

Even when divorced parents do maintain regular contact with their children,

From Karl Zinsmeister, "Divorce's Toll on Children," *American Enterprise*, May/June 1996. Reprinted by permission of the *American Enterprise*, a Washington, D.C.-based magazine of politics, business, and culture.

truly cooperative childrearing is very rare. Most often, research shows, the estranged parents have no communication or mutual reinforcement. As a result, mother and father frequently undercut each other, intentionally or not, and parent-child relations are often unhealthy.

A series of interviews with children of divorce conducted by author/photographer Jill Krementz illustrates this phenomenon. "My relationship with my parents has changed because now my mother does all the disciplining," says 14-year-old Meredith, "and sometimes she resents it—especially when we tell her how much fun we have with Dad. It's as if it's all fun and games with him because we're with him so little." Ari, also 14, confides, "I really look forward to the weekends because it's kind of like a break—it's like going to Disneyland because there's no set schedule, no 'Be home by 5:30' kind of stuff. It's open. It's free. And my father is always buying me presents." Zach, age 13, reports "whenever I want to see my other parent I can, and if I have a fight with one of them, instead of having to take off . . . I can just go eat at my Mom's house or my Dad's."

Other youngsters feel torn in two after a divorce, particularly in cases of joint custody where they must physically bounce back and forth between two houses. "It's hello, goodbye, hello, goodbye all the time," says one father. Gary Skoloff, chairman of the American Bar Association's family law section, explains that "joint custody was going to be a great panacea, the ultimate solution. . . . But it turned out to be the world's worst situation." The lack of a stable home has proved so harmful to children that several states, including California where the practice was pioneered, have recently revoked statutes favoring joint custody.

> *"Since 1972, more than a million youngsters have been involved in a divorce each year."*

Fear and Loathing of Divorce Among the Young

Children's view of divorce is unambiguous: it's a disaster. In 1988, professor Jeanne Dise-Lewis surveyed almost 700 junior high school students, asking them to rate a number of life events in terms of stressfulness. The only thing students ranked as more stressful than parental divorce was death of a parent or close family member. Parental divorce received a higher rating than the death of a friend, being "physically hit" by a parent, feeling that no one liked them, or being seriously injured.

The "fairy tale" believed by adults, says University of Michigan psychologist and divorce expert Neil Kalter, is that if they simply present new family set-ups to their children in a calm, firm way, the children will accept them. Actually, he says, that "is seen by the kids as a lot of baloney." Among the hundreds of children he's worked with in setting up coping-with-divorce programs for schools, "there are very few who have anything good to say about divorce." "Children are generally more traditional than adults," agrees Judith Wallerstein. "Children want both parents. They want family." If children had the vote, she says, there would be no such thing as divorce.

Indeed, Gallup youth surveys in the early 1990s show that three out of four teenagers age 13 to 17 think "it is too easy for people in this country to get divorced." Go into a typical high school today and ask some students what their most important wish for the future is and a surprising number will answer "that there wouldn't be so many divorces." Young Arizonan Cynthia Coan has lots of company when she says, "as a child of divorce, I cannot help but hope that the next generation of children will be spared what mine went through."

> *"If children had the vote . . . there would be no such thing as divorce."*

You'll sometimes hear the claim that divorce doesn't hurt children as much as conflict in a marriage. This is not supported by the evidence. "For kids," reports Kalter, "the misery in an unhappy marriage is usually less significant than the changes" after a divorce. "They'd rather their parents keep fighting and not get divorced." Even five years later, few of the youngsters in Wallerstein's study agreed with their parents' decision to separate. Only 10 percent were more content after the split than before.

Children's Best Interests?

Contrary to popular perceptions, the alternative to most divorces is not life in a war zone. Though more than 50 percent of all marriages currently end in divorce, experts tell us that only about 15 percent of all unions involve high levels of conflict. In the vast number of divorces, then, there is no gross strife or violence that could warp a youngster's childhood. The majority of marital breakups are driven by a quest for greener grass—and in these cases the children will almost always be worse off.

Many mothers and fathers badly underestimate how damaging household dissolution will be to their children. A 1985 British study that quizzed both parents and children found that the children reported being far more seriously upset by their parents' separation than the parents assumed. Despite the common perception that the best thing parents can do for their children is to make themselves happy, the truth is that children have their own needs that exist quite apart from those of their parents. One may argue that a parent should be allowed to rank his own needs above those of his children (though this is not the traditional understanding of how families should work). But one ought not cloak that decision with the false justification that one is thereby serving the children's best interests.

Wade Horn, former commissioner of the U.S. Administration for Children, Youth, and Families, illustrates how parents can be deluded in this way:

Families used to come to me when I was practicing psychology, seeking advice about how to divorce. They would say, "We want a divorce because we really don't get along very well any more, and we understand that our child will be better off after we divorce than if we stay together." Rarely, if ever, did I hear a family say, "We're having conflict, but we have decided to work as hard as we can at solving our problems because we know that children of divorce are more disturbed than children of intact families."

A major reason parents are making this mistake is because that is what some authorities and many ideologues in the cause of family "liberation" have been telling them. "For years experts said, 'Once the initial trauma wears off, kids make adjustments,'" complains psychologist John Guidubaldi, past president of the National Association of School Psychologists. While it's true that kids make adjustments, Guidubaldi notes in the *Washington Post*, "so do people in prisons and mental institutions. The pertinent question is: Are those adjustments healthy? And the weight of the evidence has become overwhelming on the side that they aren't."

Short- and Long-Term Effects of Divorce on Children

The longer-term effects of divorce on children are something we've learned a lot about over the last decade. Guidubaldi, who orchestrated one of the large studies documenting these effects, concludes from his work that "the old argument of staying together for the sake of the kids is still the best argument. . . . People simply aren't putting enough effort into saving their marriages." Family scholar Nicholas Zill points out that "if you looked at the kind of long-term risk factors that divorce creates for kids and translated them to, say, heart disease, people would be startled."

In the early months after divorce, young children are often less imaginative and more repetitive. Many become passive watchers. They tend to be more dependent, demanding, unaffectionate, and disobedient than their counterparts from intact families. They are more afraid of abandonment, loss of love, and bodily harm. A significant number—in some studies a quarter—say they blame themselves for their parents' smash-up.

> *"Many mothers and fathers badly underestimate how damaging household dissolution will be to their children."*

A small study conducted some years ago by University of Hawaii psychiatrist John McDermott sorted pre-schoolers who had been involved in a divorce a few months earlier into three categories. Three out of 16 children were judged to have weathered the initial storm essentially unchanged. Two of 16 became what he called "severely disorganized" and developed gross behavior problems. The rest, more than two-thirds, he categorized as "the sad, angry children." They displayed resentment, depression, and grief, were restless, noisy, possessive, and physically aggressive.

In Judith Wallerstein's landmark study, almost half of the pre-schoolers still displayed heightened anxiety and aggression a full year after their parents' divorce. Forty-four percent "were found to be in significantly deteriorated psychological condition." All of the two- and three-year-olds showed acute regression in toilet training. They displayed unusual hunger for attention from strangers. Older pre-schoolers had become more whiny, irritable, and aggressive, and had problems with play.

> *"A significant number [of children of divorce] say they blame themselves for their parents' smash-up."*

Wallerstein's study also returned to its subjects five and 10 years later, and the collected results are quite staggering. In overview they look like this: initially, two-thirds of all the children showed symptoms of stress, and half thought their life had been destroyed by the divorce. Five years down the road, over a third were still seriously disturbed (even more disturbed than they had been initially, in fact), and another third were having psychological difficulties. A surprisingly large number remained angry at their parents.

After a decade, 45 percent of the children were doing well, 14 percent were succeeding in some areas but failing in others, and 41 percent were still doing quite poorly. This last group "were entering adulthood as worried, underachieving, self-deprecating, and sometimes angry young men and women." In addition to their emotional problems and depression, many felt sorrow over their childhoods and fear about their own marriage and childrearing prospects. About a third of the group had little or no ambition at the 10-year mark. Many expressed a sense of powerlessness, neediness, and vulnerability. Most of the ones who had reached adult age regarded their parents' divorce as a continuing major influence in their lives.

It should be noted that the 131 children in the study experienced divorce in what Wallerstein and associates call the "best of circumstances." Most of their parents were college educated, and at the beginning these children were achievers in school. None of the participants was initially being treated for psychiatric disorder. Most of the families were white and middle class; half regularly attended church or synagogue.

Behavioral Changes Among Children of Divorce

Even in families with all these advantages, divorce wreaks havoc among the young. Summarizing her findings on the offspring of broken marriages, Wallerstein has written that "it would be hard to find any other group of children—except, perhaps, the victims of a natural disaster—who suffered such a rate of sudden serious psychological problems." Other long-term studies reach similar conclusions. "Divorce," says psychiatrist McDermott, "is now the single largest cause of childhood depression." Marital disruption, quite clearly, can wound children for years.

Let's look more specifically at some of the changes in behavior that affect children of divorce. John Guidubaldi and Joseph Perry found in their survey of 700 youngsters that children of divorced parents performed worse than children of intact families on nine of 30 mental health measures, showing, among other things, more withdrawal, dependency, inattention, and unhappiness, plus less work effort. Divorced students were more likely to abuse drugs, to commit violent acts, to take their own life, and to bear children out of wedlock.

A University of Pittsburgh study in the late 1980s found that there were 30 percent more duodenal ulcers and 70 percent more suicide attempts—both symptoms of serious psychological stress—among children who had lost a parent. In Wallerstein's middle-class sample, one-third of the girls with divorced parents became pregnant out of wedlock, and 8 percent had at least two abortions. Two-thirds of the girls had a history of delinquency, and almost 30 percent of the boys had been arrested more than once.

The National Survey of Children showed that more than 30 percent of the individuals whose parents separated or divorced before they were eight years old had received therapy by the time they were teenagers. Divorce-children are two to four times as numerous in psychiatric care populations as they are in society at large. In fact, more than 80 percent of the adolescents in mental hospitals, and 60 percent of the children in psychiatric clinics, have been through a divorce. And what is being treated in most cases is much more than just a short-term reaction: the average treatment takes place five years after their parents' marital break-up. At the fully adult age of 23, middle-class women whose mother and father had divorced were three times likelier to have a psychological problem than counterparts from intact families, according to a massive multi-year British study.

> *"Divorce . . . is now the single largest cause of childhood depression."*

Schooling is another problem area. Children exposed to divorce are twice as likely to repeat a grade, and five times likelier to be expelled or suspended. (Fully 15 percent of all teenagers living with divorced mothers have been booted from school at least temporarily, according to the National Survey of Children.) Even in Wallerstein's middle-class sample, 13 percent of the youngsters had dropped out of school altogether. Barely half of Wallerstein's subjects went on to college, far less than the 85 percent average for students in their high schools. Wallerstein concludes that 60 percent of the divorce-children in her study will fail to match the educational achievements of their fathers.

Children of divorce also frequently have problems with sexual identity. In most studies, boys seem to be harder hit than girls. Pre-school boys tend to be unpopular with male peers, to have difficulty gaining access to play groups, to spend more time with younger compatriots and females, and to engage in more activities traditionally considered to be feminine. Young boys tend to be more vehemently opposed to the divorce, to long more for their father, to feel rejected by him, and to feel uncertain about their masculinity. They are more likely than girls to become depressed and angry. Many later have problems developing intimacy, and build lifestyles of solitary interests and habits.

For girls there is a "sleeper effect"—beginning at adolescence, seemingly well-adjusted individuals often develop serious problems with sexuality, self-control, and intimacy. Kalter found higher rates of substance abuse, running away, and sexual activity among girls who had been through divorce, particularly when the father had departed early on. Wallerstein found that a "significant minority" of girls expressed insecurity, anger, or lack of self-respect in promiscuity, some gravitating to older men or a series of aimless sexual relationships. "I'm prepared for anything. I don't expect a lot," said one 20-year-old. "Love is a strange idea to me. Life is a chess game. I've always been a pawn."

Divorce Affects Relationships Later in Life

Mavis Hetherington of the University of Virginia has found that girls have special problems when their divorced mothers remarry. She has also shown that the pattern of low self-respect and sexual precocity among girls with a divorced mother does *not* hold true among girls living with a solo mother due to death of the father—apparently it is active alienation from the father, more than his simple absence, that causes the disturbance. This fits well with psychologist Erik Erikson's view that it is less deprivation *per se* that is psychologically destructive than deprivation without redeeming significance.

Wallerstein points out that teenage girls often view their absent fathers with a combination of idealization and distrust.

> The idealized father that the young adolescent girl imagines is the exact opposite of the image that later becomes prominent in her mind as she grows older—namely, the father as betrayer. . . . Because daughters of divorce often have a hard time finding out what their fathers are really like, they often experience great difficulty in establishing a realistic view of men in general, in developing realistic expectations, and in exercising good judgment in their choice of partner.

Researcher Conrad Schwarz has hypothesized that children who are allied only with their same-sex parent (as a girl growing up with a divorced mother would be) tend to hold a chauvinistic and alienated view of the opposite sex. Conversely, he suggests, children growing up with only opposite-sex parents (like boys living

> *"Divorce-children are two to four times as numerous in psychiatric care populations as they are in society at large."*

with divorced mothers) tend to have problems with gender identity and self-esteem. One study that fits this hypothesis found that college-age women who had experienced divorce in childhood were more prone to see men as unfeeling and weak than counterparts from intact families.

Female children of divorced parents are more likely to choose "inadequate husbands" and to have marital problems of their own. They are substantially likelier to have extensive premarital sexual experience and twice as likely to cohabit before marriage. They are more frequently pregnant at their weddings.

And both male and female children of divorce see their own marriages dissolve at significantly higher rates than counterparts who grew up in intact families. Partly this is attitudinal: One eight-year study of 1,300 men and women found that people who had watched their own parents divorce were much more tolerant of the idea of divorce, and that this tolerance translated into increased marital break-up.

The other thing that childhood divorce encourages, of course, is the avoidance of marriage. "My mom got remarried and divorced again, so I've gone through two divorces so far. And my father's also gotten remarried—to someone I don't get along with all that well. It's all made me feel that people shouldn't get married," 14-year-old Ari explained to Jill Krementz.

Divorces involving children thus set a whole train of losses into motion, transporting unhappy effects not only over the years but even across generations. And not even children fortunate enough to live in stable homes are wholly insulated from the turmoil. As writer Susan Cohen observes:

> Although I am not divorced and live in a conventional nuclear family with a husband and two children . . . divorce has been part of my daughter Sarah's life since she was two or three. Divorce is in her books, on her television programs, in her lessons at school, in her conversations with her friends, and in her questions to me.

Indeed, divorce is in the very air our children breathe—with lasting significance for their later views of love, families, and life.

Multiple Divorce Harms Children

by Susan Chira

About the author: *Susan Chira is a freelance journalist.*

First, Annie and Ivan married.

They had two children. They divorced. Later, Barry moved into Annie's house. Annie loved him. Her children did not. Three years passed, and he was gone. Two years later, Annie moved her children into Lee's house. Annie loved him. Her children did not.

For nearly three years, Annie and Lee and her children have circled one another warily, trying to decide whether this newest family could endure.

Annie's children, like countless across the country, are part of an increasingly common American family—the one that is formed, shattered, reformed and shattered again in the wake of repeated divorces and breakups. These children struggle to navigate a bewildering succession of stepparents, stepsiblings and live-in relationships that have no formal name.

Researchers who follow these children say their ranks are swelling and their lives are often rocky. Studies comparing families of multiple divorce with families of single divorces have found that children with more family disruptions report higher levels of anxiety and depression, worse academic records and more troubled marriages of their own. The more breakups children experience, the studies show, the worse they fare.

"You get cumulative effects," said Lawrence A. Kurdek, a professor of psychology at Wright State University in Dayton, Ohio, and the author of one such study. "You're losing or gaining a lot more than a parent; you're changing households, schools, friends. The kids get rooted; they get uprooted. Their overall sense of stability has got to be pretty shaky."

Half of all marriages end in divorce, and even more remarriages fall apart. Frank F. Furstenberg Jr. and Andrew J. Cherlin, two leading divorce researchers, estimate that 15 percent of all children in divorced families will see the parent they live with remarry and redivorce before they reach age 18. And that figure is a conservative estimate, they say, because it does not include couples who live together instead of remarry.

A Multiple-Divorce Family

Annie P. and Lee S., who now share a home on a tree-lined street in a middle-class suburb in northern New Jersey, illustrate the trends the demographers are tracking. Like all the people mentioned in this viewpoint, their full names are not given so as to protect their children's privacy. Like other parents with several breakups in their past, Annie and Lee have presided uneasily over their stepfamily, one forged by affection, haunted by old relationships and buffeted by the resentments of children who have seen past families come and go.

"We start meeting all the cousins and brothers and daughters, and it's kind of a pain," said Michelle, Annie's 18-year-old daughter, who is in her first year at a college in upstate New York. "You have such an extended family. I thought it was kind of embarrassing to go to events—'I'm the new girl-friend's daughter.' And then, let's say we do make a relationship with one of the children or something, as soon as Mom breaks up with this guy, that has to be killed."

Researchers caution that much of the damage of single or repeated divorces depends on factors that are hard to measure: how much conflict dogged the relationship and the

"The more breakups children experience, the studies show, the worse they fare."

breakup, how much continuity parents are able to preserve in children's lives and how well parents who are bruised themselves are able to help their children. And while most children of multiple divorces are not consigned to bleak fates, the upheavals take their toll.

"I had a lot of anger building up," said David, Annie's 13-year-old son, re-counting his resentment at being moved from his old town and into Lee's home. "Punching the pillow doesn't help me. Writing something doesn't help me either. I need to say how I feel."

Michelle and David are calmer now after years of emotional turmoil. They speak of their mother with deep loyalty and affection, even as they say they did not like the men she brought into their lives.

Annie, meanwhile, has struggled to balance her responsibilities to her children with her own need for companionship. She has raised Michelle and David virtually on her own, with small financial contributions and periodic visits from their father. She has managed to get free therapy for them, agreed to a rabbi's bargain that she attend adult Jewish education classes in return for free Hebrew school for them, and forged close ties with their teachers.

"You have kids you have to be responsible for," said Annie, 43, a trim, vibrant woman with expressive eyes. "You have to make decisions that go beyond your own personal needs. But you also can't let them dictate whether you should be in a relationship or you shouldn't."

The First Breakup

Michelle and David were 8 and 3 years old when the first family they knew broke apart in 1984, in a long, wrenching divorce. A judge ordered their father, Ivan P., out of his wife's bedroom but not out of the house.

"It was the court system that was at fault," Annie said. "You don't order a man out of his bedroom and not expect there's going to be a war." Her husband never hit her, Annie said, but she recalls times when he backed her into a corner in a menacing way. For two years, Annie and Ivan tried futilely to shield their battles from their children.

"He was living downstairs and she was upstairs," Michelle said. "It was very confusing as to what was going on. To this day I remember we were downstairs moving the piano. His temper just went off. That always stuck in my head."

In the end, Annie, ill with pneumonia and worried that her children were suffering too much, decided to settle out of court. "My eyes were open all night," Annie said of that time. "There are so many people's lives in your hands at that moment. What if you make a mistake? It is not just you. That's what makes you compromise. The kids always take precedence."

For more and more American children, as for Michelle and David, the first family breakup in their young lives is not their last. Larry Bumpass, a demographer at the University of Wisconsin, has assembled the most comprehensive data on divorce and cohabitation through a national survey of households and families he has been conducting since 1987.

The Growing Number of Multiple-Divorce Families

Neither he nor other researchers can say exactly how many children experience multiple family breakups because few researchers have tracked cohabitation on a national level. But Professor Bumpass says he believes their numbers are swelling. Remarriages have a greater chance of breaking up than first marriages. He found that 37 percent of remarriages collapsed within 10 years, compared with 30 percent of first marriages in that period of time. Moreover, nearly one-third of American children are born to unmarried mothers, and many will see their families split, reform and split again, he said.

> *"For more and more American children . . . the first family breakup in their young lives is not their last."*

After the divorce, Michelle and David continued to see their father, whom they speak of fondly although they say their mother is the one they confide in. The children mourned the separation not only from their father, but also from his daughter by a previous marriage, who had been a frequent visitor in their home.

Annie took her children to see a therapist, joining an experimental program to save money. Michelle had grown clingy and very frightened, striving to be the peacemaker and feeling responsible for her mother and brother. Therapy seemed to help Michelle more than David, who remained angry at his mother and prone to outbursts of hostility in nursery school. Annie met with each child's teachers each year, telling them about the divorce and asking them to be her eyes and ears while she worked.

The Second Breakup

Not long after her divorce from Ivan, Annie met Joel F., a divorced father of two children. They dated for two years. Michelle and David liked Joel and his children, but the relationship did not last.

While Annie said she was conscious of the need to keep her personal life separate from her children, she could not always do so. "I tried to shield as much as possible," she said. "There were a lot of dates my kids never met. But if you're divorced and kids are living with you, baby sitters are very expensive and you can't leave the kids alone. It forced me to introduce men to my children sooner."

Then Annie fell in love with Barry L., who moved in with her. For a single mother exhausted by working full time and raising two children, Barry meant companionship, support, a novel lightheartedness. "He had the gift of being able to make me laugh," she said.

> *"Children who have seen several families fall apart often wrestle with feelings of distrust, anxiety and betrayal, researchers say."*

Annie remembers golden times, when Barry took David hunting or when the two worked for months on an elaborate castle complete with small warriors and horses, a castle that Annie has packed up in the basement so David can pass it on to his children.

But she knows that her children remember a different, harsher Barry. "He was kind of a tough guy," David said. "He wouldn't allow my sister and I to be with my mother in her room. He'd lock the door and keep us out. Before, we'd hang out in her room and watch movies. When he came, that just stopped."

When their mother was not around, Michelle said, Barry would shout at them. When Annie asked Barry to move out after three years, Michelle and her brother spent no time crying over that breakup. "Oh yeah," Michelle said, "it was just great."

Children who have seen several families fall apart often wrestle with feelings of distrust, anxiety and betrayal, researchers say.

Repeated divorces or breakups appear to worsen the well-documented consequences of divorce, when parents typically spend less time with children and when the family income typically drops. Regardless of their parents' educational backgrounds, these children are more likely than those who grew up with two biological parents to drop out of high school, play truant and earn lower grades and test scores. They also have fewer expectations of attending college.

In a nationwide study of 1,243 people tracked since 1980, Paul R. Amato of the University of Nebraska and Alan Booth of Pennsylvania State University found in 1991 that those who experienced multiple divorces reported higher levels of anxiety and depression as adults and had more troubled marriages and higher divorce rates.

"Those who counsel children of multiple divorce say that the trauma of forming a new stepfamily . . . may be harder on children than a subsequent breakup."

In a study of fifth- and sixth-graders in two Midwestern cities published in 1994, Professor Kurdek, Mark A. Fine and Ronald J. Sinclair found that children of repeated divorces earned lower grades and lower approval ratings from their own peers. In the nationwide study and in this one however, the difference between the children of multiple and single divorces was small.

Those who counsel children of multiple divorce say that the trauma of forming a new stepfamily, with a stranger intruding on their time with a parent, may be harder on children than a subsequent breakup.

"When they were living with Mom, it was 'You're my best buddy,'" said Elizabeth McGonagle, a social worker in Ballston Spa, N.Y., who founded Banana Splits, a peer support group for children of divorce that has been used around the country. "Then along comes Prince Charming and the child all of a sudden has to go to bed on time."

The Third Breakup

In 1991, a year after Barry moved out of Annie's house, Annie met Lee S., a businessman who had just weathered his second divorce. Lee brought his own ghosts to the relationship. His first marriage, which lasted 17 years, had produced three children, and he was stepfather to two children during his second, 11-year-marriage.

After a year of dating, with an engagement ring on her finger and Lee's promise to marry within a few months, Annie moved her children into the home where Lee had lived with his second wife. Her children not only clashed with Lee, but also hated leaving their old friends and schools. And they had minimal contact with Lee's children.

"My mom gave me a choice of staying in my school but said the new school would be the only way of making friends in a new town," Michelle said. "But it was my junior year in high school, and I didn't meet people. This switch was just horrendous. I cried all the time to her."

Sara McLanahan, a leading divorce researcher at Princeton University, has identified moving as one of the most damaging effects of divorce for children.

In *Growing Up with a Single Parent: What Hurts, What Helps*, one of the most comprehensive statistical overviews of the consequences of divorce and single parenthood, Professor McLanahan and Gary Sandefur conclude that up to 40 percent of the increased risk of becoming a high school dropout is attributable to moving as a result of divorce. That is because children lose invaluable ties to friends, teachers and neighbors that may help buffer the split from a parent.

Michelle and David were not only feeling uprooted by the move, but they also had a stormy relationship with Lee and resented his attempts to discipline them. Lee balked at what he saw as the children's insolence to their mother. "We had different perceptions of child-rearing," Annie said. "Lee came into my family with the perception that children are respectful, follow directions and are disciplined, whereas my belief is that children need to be heard."

Family Conflict

David found himself in trouble at home with Lee and at school. "I was just confused," David said. "As soon as a teacher snapped at me, I just couldn't take it anymore. I don't like my school. I don't like this town at all. I want to move very badly. Everything was building up, how I hate the town, my problems with my family. I couldn't concentrate."

Michelle withdrew. "It got to the point I wanted to move out of the house," she said. "I didn't even look at him."

Annie said she had to become stricter with her children in order to satisfy Lee. But she also accused Lee of trying to impose his authority too soon, and the tension corroded their relationship as well.

"He didn't feel that he comes first," she said. "My children come first. That caused a lot of conflict for us as a couple and a family—jealousy, anger, blame. I'm the one in the middle. I get blamed for everything. You blame yourself on top of that. I would find myself constantly thinking about what's the right thing to do. I would tear myself inside out driving, dealing with business, thinking about what to do."

Lee put off the wedding twice, Annie said, partly because of their conflicts about the children. After one particularly bad fight in 1994, Annie's children confronted her with a choice: Lee or them. "I felt the answer did not lie in giving into any ultimatum on either side," Annie said, "but to work out the differences."

> *"Up to 40 percent of the increased risk of becoming a high school dropout is attributable to moving as a result of divorce."*

But after months of fighting, Annie decided . . . to break up with Lee. . . .

Michelle talks of pain and confusion, but she has emerged strong and confident—thanks, she says, to her close bond to her mother. She looks back with devotion and exasperation. "The thing I didn't like was that she never asked our permission or what we thought of it,

77

like Barry's moving in or we're going to live at Lee's house," she said. "I don't think children should go through divorce to mature. But I think it's helped me as far as becoming independent. There's a lot of things I've either been through or can handle that a lot of my peers are oblivious to."

David sounds more wistful than angry. "I think I'd be a lot happier if things were the way they had been at the beginning," he said. "Oh, I don't even know that. I just remember when it was just me, my sister and my mom. I remember things were fine then."

The Harmful Effects of Divorce Have Been Exaggerated

by Barbara Ehrenreich

About the author: *Barbara Ehrenreich is a freelance writer.*

No one seems much concerned about children when the subject is welfare or Medicaid cuts, but mention divorce, and tears flow for their tender psyches. Legislators in half a dozen states are planning to restrict divorce on the grounds that it may cause teen suicide, an inability to "form lasting attachments" and possibly also the piercing of nipples and noses.

But if divorce itself hasn't reduced America's youth to emotional cripples, then the efforts to restrict it undoubtedly will. First, there's the effect all this antidivorce rhetoric is bound to have on the children of people already divorced—and we're not talking about some offbeat minority. At least 37% of American children live with divorced parents, and these children already face enough tricky interpersonal situations without having to cope with the public perception that they're damaged goods.

Fortunately for the future of the republic, the alleged psyche-scarring effects of divorce have been grossly exaggerated. The most frequently cited study, by California therapist Judith Wallerstein, found that 41% of the children of divorced couples are "doing poorly, worried, underachieving, deprecating and often angry" years after their parents' divorce. But this study has been faulted for including only 60 couples, two-thirds of whom were deemed to lack "adequate psychological functioning" even before they split, and all of whom were self-selected seekers of family therapy. Furthermore, there was no control group of, say, miserable couples who stayed together.

As for some of the wilder claims, such as "teen suicide has tripled as divorces have tripled": well, roller-blading has probably tripled in the same time period too, and that's hardly a reason to ban in-line skates.

In fact, the current antidivorce rhetoric slanders millions of perfectly wonderful, high-functioning young people, my own children and most of their friends included. Studies that attempt to distinguish between the effects of divorce and those of the income decline so often experienced by divorced mothers have found no lasting psychological damage attributable to divorce per se. Check out a typical college dorm, and you'll find people enthusiastically achieving and forming attachments until late into the night. Ask about family, and you'll hear about Mom and Dad . . . and Stepmom and Stepdad.

The real problems for kids will begin when the antidivorce movement starts getting its way. For one thing, the more militant among its members want to "re-stigmatize" divorce with the cultural equivalent of a scarlet *D*. Sadly though, divorce is already stigmatized in ways that are harmful to children. Studies show that teachers consistently interpret children's behavior more negatively when they are told that the children are from "broken" homes—and, as we know, teachers' expectations have an effect on children's performance. If the idea is to help the children of divorce, then the goal should be to *de*-stigmatize divorce among all who interact with them—teachers, neighbors, playmates.

Then there are the likely effects on children of the proposed restrictions themselves. Antidivorce legislators want to repeal no-fault divorce laws and return to the system in which one parent has to prove the other guilty of adultery, addiction or worse. True, the divorce rate rose after the introduction of no-fault divorce in the late '60s and '70s. But the divorce rate was already rising at a healthy clip *before* that, so there's no guarantee that the repeal of no-fault laws will reduce the divorce rate now. In fact, one certain effect will be to generate more divorces of the rancorous, potentially child-harming variety. If you think "Mommy and Daddy aren't getting along" sounds a little too blithe, would you rather "Daddy (or Mommy) has been sleeping around"?

> *"Fortunately for the future of the republic, the alleged psyche-scarring effects of divorce have been grossly exaggerated."*

Not that divorce is an enviable experience for any of the parties involved. But just as there are bad marriages, there are, as sociologist Constance Ahrons argues, "good divorces," in which both parents maintain their financial and emotional responsibility for the kids. Maybe the reformers should concentrate on improving the *quality* of divorces—by, for example, requiring prenuptial agreements specifying how the children will be cared for in the event of a split.

The antidivorce movement's interest in the emotional status of children would be more convincing if it were linked to some concern for their physical survival. The most destructive feature of divorce, many experts argue, is the poverty that typically ensues when the children are left with a low-earning mother, and the way out of this would be to toughen child-support collection and strengthen the safety net of supportive services for low-income families—

including childcare, Medicaid and welfare.

Too difficult? Too costly? Too ideologically distasteful compared with denouncing divorce and, by implication, the divorced and their children? Perhaps. But sometimes grownups have to do difficult and costly things, whether they feel like doing them or not. For the sake of the children, that is.

Divorce Does Not Necessarily Harm Children

by Andrew J. Cherlin

About the author: *Andrew J. Cherlin is a sociology professor at Johns Hopkins University in Baltimore, Maryland.*

In his 1992 *Public Interest* article entitled "For the Sake of the Children," Richard Gill criticizes a study several collaborators and I published in 1991 on the effects of divorce on children. Gill first charges that our methodology and our interpretation are flawed, then launches into a broader discussion of contemporary marriage and divorce. In a 1991 *Public Interest* article, "Day Care or Parental Care?", Gill expressed similar concerns about the direction of family policy and the well-being of American children.

Gill's concern about children is well-founded, and we share it. It was never our intent to conduct a study that would absolve divorcing parents of guilt. In our current research, in fact, we have found some harmful effects of divorce on young children who were assessed shortly after their parents' marriages broke up. Nevertheless, we think that Gill's procedural criticisms are groundless and, more important, that the underlying themes of both his articles are unhelpful as a guide to public policy concerning children and families. In this viewpoint, I will address Gill's specific criticisms and then respond more generally to his two articles.

For our study of divorce, we analyzed statistics from two surveys, one British and one American, that had followed national samples of children and their families for several years. We identified about 12,000 seven-year-old British children and 800 seven- to eleven-year-old American children whose parents were married at the beginning of the survey period, and we tracked these children for the next four to five years. Not surprisingly, children whose parents separated or divorced displayed more behavior problems and performed more poorly in school than children whose parents remained married. But when we looked back to the beginnings of the surveys, we found that the children—par-

From Andrew J. Cherlin, "Nostalgia as Family Policy." Reprinted, with permission, from the *Public Interest*, no. 110, Winter 1993; ©1993, National Affairs, Inc.

ticularly boys—whose parents were then married but would later divorce were *already* displaying more behavior problems and performing more poorly in school than the children whose parents would remain married. We concluded:

> Overall, the evidence suggests that much of the effect of divorce on children can be predicted by conditions that existed well before the separation occurred. . . . [T]he British and U.S. longitudinal studies suggest that those concerned with the effects of divorce on children should consider reorienting their thinking. At least as much attention needs to be paid to the processes that occur in troubled, intact families as to the trauma that children suffer after their parents separate.

Disputed Survey Data

Although Gill agrees with our call for more attention to troubled, intact families, he disputes our conclusion that much of the harm experienced by children of divorce is due to conditions that exist before separation occurs. He notes that the British study, by far the larger of the two, followed children from 1965 to 1969, when the divorce rate was much lower than it is today. Only 11 percent of British children during that period experienced a divorce before they were sixteen, compared to about 40 percent of U.S. children today. The social climate in Great Britain, Gill argues, must have been more favorable for keeping marriages together and making them work. Gill then goes on to make the crucial assumption—without any evidence—that a high proportion of those British marriages ending in divorce must have been "very troubled." He speculates that these marriages were characterized by "physical, sexual, or psychological abuses, whether directed toward child or spouse, that not only justify but clearly mandate separation and divorce." No wonder, he concludes, that the British children were often troubled before the separation—only deeply troubled families got divorced.

But were the British marriages that ended in divorce much more troubled than American marriages that end in divorce today? Although we cannot be sure, we doubt it for two reasons. First, we deleted from our British study all families in which separation occurred before the child's seventh birthday. We did this because the interviews conducted with the parents and teachers of seven-year-olds in intact families provided us with the first detailed family information that could serve as a pre-separation benchmark. A fortuitous

> *"Much of the effect of divorce on children can be predicted by conditions that existed well before the separation occurred."*

result is that couples whose marriages lasted fewer than seven years were excluded. In fact, we excluded more divorced couples than we retained. We think it very likely that seriously troubled, abusive marriages tend to break up more quickly than marriages with more minor sources of conflict. If so, then the families we retained are probably more like contemporary families than Gill believes.

Second, each interview with the parent of a seven-year-old was conducted by a Local Authority Health Visitor, a trained nurse employed by the municipality, who normally visited each mother before her child was born and returned afterward, often several times if the family was experiencing problems. The Health Visitor's questionnaire included a checklist that noted any family difficulties or use of social-welfare services. Relatively few problems were noted for the families

> *"American boys, just like British ones, showed many behavior problems before their parents divorced."*

that later divorced. Health Visitors checked "domestic tension" for 17 percent of later-divorced families, "financial difficulties" for 16 percent, contact with the child-welfare department for 8 percent, mental illness or neurosis for 7 percent, and alcoholism for 1 percent. To be sure, the Health Visitors may have been unaware of many problems. Still, the reports do not suggest that these families were in great conflict.

Pre- and Post-Divorce Behavior Problems

Our American survey data were recent enough (1976 to 1981) that Gill could not contend they were collected in an era of lower divorce. Yet we found that American boys, just like British ones, showed many behavior problems before their parents divorced. In the case of American girls, we found that once we controlled for pre-divorce problems they showed modestly better behavior if their parents divorced than if they stayed together. It is understandable that Gill seizes upon this puzzling finding for girls as evidence that our American results are flawed. Yet the gender difference did not surprise clinicians who deal with children. Several leading studies of divorce have found what appear to be greater effects on boys than on girls. In fact, a twelve-year longitudinal study of children in Berkeley, California, found that girls whose families experienced high levels of conflict showed fewer outward signs of problems than girls in less troubled families. Developmental psychologist Robert E. Emery writes in *Marriage, Divorce, and Children's Adjustment* that girls sometimes react to the stress of divorce by displaying over-controlled, "good" behavior. These girls are, indeed, distressed by the divorce, according to Emery, but they respond to their distress by trying to help out and be accommodating. In divorce—and in reaction to other sources of stress—girls tend to internalize their distress, which makes it difficult to observe. Boys, on the other hand, externalize their distress through obvious misbehavior. Thus, our American findings are consistent with the observations of developmental and clinical psychologists.

Gill also presents a table from a recent American study showing that children from disrupted families experienced more difficulties, but that study did not take into account what the children's families were like before the disruptions.

The Emotional Costs of Divorce

Yet Gill's discussion extends far beyond our article and the procedures we followed. He argues that living in a high-divorce-rate society leads couples to focus more on self-fulfillment and less on keeping their marriages together, to the detriment of children:

> According to this argument, divorce involves an important externality. My divorce affects not only my own children but also, by adding to the divorce rate, the dysfunction and conflict in other marriages and hence the welfare of children in other families.

The claim here is that in a high-divorce-rate society spouses feel freer to argue because they know divorce is an option if they can't resolve their differences. The opposite position could, of course, be argued: that in a high-divorce-rate society there is less conflict in marriages because couples that can't get along divorce. Moreover, it is possible that one couple's divorce could make other couples *less* likely to divorce. Studies show that adults who divorce experience considerable anguish and distress; even those who initiate a divorce often report feelings of loss, sadness, and anger for years. The married friends of persons who divorce witness this distress, are often asked to provide comfort, and therefore learn how difficult a divorce is. A greater awareness of the emotional and economic costs of divorce may be one reason why the U.S. divorce rate has declined about 10 percent from its 1981 peak.

> *"It is possible that one couple's divorce could make other couples* less *likely to divorce."*

Dissatisfied Wives Pay a Price

I could not find any hard evidence about whether there was less conflict in marriages when divorce rates were lower a few decades ago; nor does Gill cite any evidence. His assertion remains an open question. Nevertheless, intrigued by his argument, I examined the historical literature on the American family in the 1950s. For example, historian Elaine Tyler May, in *Homeward Bound: American Families in the Cold War Era*, studied the records of 300 middle-class couples who were interviewed extensively in 1955. These couples, as Gill would predict, did indeed try to stifle their anger and avoid conflict so that their marriages would stay together. But the interviews also suggest that the suppression of conflict came at a price—and that wives paid that price.

When the wives were asked to evaluate their marriages, they first listed the benefits: economic security, a nice home, children, companionship. Yet they were twice as likely as their husbands to report that they were dissatisfied with their marriages, and twice as many said they would not marry the same person if they had it to do over again. Many stayed in their marriages despite hardship, strain, and bitterness. One wife wrote:

One particular source of friction: My husband is a firm believer in "woman's place is in the home"—so it is, to a degree—but I have always felt the need for outside activities and interest in community affairs because I felt mentally stagnant by not taking part in outside programs and because I feel morally obligated to take part, in view of my education and some capabilities. He takes no interest in my interests and belittles most women's groups. . . . Whatever I have done has had to be at no inconvenience to him—and often with a scornful attitude on his part.

Another wrote:

Much of our trouble has centered around my husband's unwillingness to do work around the house, which he says is my sole responsibility. . . . This was not too bad until I had the third baby within five years. . . . I became so exhausted that I got very little sleep, even when [the new baby] did, and I had to be up early with the other two little ones. . . . I believe I had a nervous breakdown but I knew psychiatric help would be expensive and my husband said, "Your trouble is all in your head and you don't have to feel this way if you don't want to."

Nevertheless, imbued with 1950s family morality, this woman said she never considered divorce, never regretted her marriage, and considered it "decidedly more happy than average." There is no record in the book of the impact of her distress on her children.

If these records are representative, it appears the lower divorce rates of the 1950s were achieved not by greater marital bliss but rather by a rigid division of labor that hid the substantial stress and frustration that many women experienced. This is hardly an original thesis—it was the message of Betty Friedan's 1963 book, *The Feminine Mystique*. Yet the 1950s was the decade in which family life came closest to Gill's ideals. For one thing, the divorce rate was substantially lower then. For another, far fewer married women worked outside the home while they were raising children.

> *"The lower divorce rates of the 1950s were achieved not by greater marital bliss but rather by a rigid division of labor that hid the . . . frustration that many women experienced."*

Gill's preference for the breadwinner-homemaker family is even more explicit in his 1991 article on day care, in which he criticizes a report of the National Research Council's Panel on Child Care Policy (of which I was a member). That report called for more government support for out-of-home child care and for work leaves for infant care. Gill argues instead for greater government support for stay-at-home parents.

Should Women Make Sacrifices?

I realize that there is no monolithic conservative position on family policy and, for that matter, that Gill may not consider himself a conservative. But his positions exemplify the main themes of conservative writings on this issue. The great contribution of conservatives in the 1970s and 1980s was to focus attention on the effects of changes in the family on children's well-being at a time when liberals were inclined to defend every kind of family and to endorse individualism uncritically. But if the strength of conservatives has been their diagnosis, their weakness is their prescription. Today, conservative observers, largely male, rightly decry the decline in children's well-being, correctly state that sacrifices will be required if the situation is to be improved, and then announce that women should make these sacrifices.

> *"Shaming, and even impoverishing women into staying married . . . seems to make up virtually the entire conservative program."*

In his article on divorce, for example, Gill outlines the potential drawbacks of plans that would combine tougher child-support enforcement with a guaranteed minimum benefit for custodial parents (usually mothers) who are owed support. Here is a measure that would force fathers to be financially responsible for their children, cut welfare costs (since the government would keep most of the payments collected from fathers if the mothers were on welfare), and provide an income floor for millions of children whose standard of living plummets after their parents divorce. What could be wrong with this plan? It would reduce the economic risk of divorce for the mother, writes Gill. This could make wives "more willing to divorce, since more financial security after divorce is now assured." And so a promising measure that would undoubtedly raise the standard of living of large numbers of children and that, as Gill acknowledges, "could conceivably render husbands more averse to divorce," is implicitly criticized because it might increase women's economic independence. . . .

Those who judge it fair to ask women to make most of the sacrifices need to ask themselves whether there is any real possibility that millions of employed women can be enticed—or even pushed—to stay at home. The economic reality is that men's wages have remained stagnant since the oil-price shocks of 1973. During the same period, housing prices have increased. For better or worse, many couples are convinced that two incomes are necessary to live the American dream. And for better or worse, the American economy depends on the services of the women who have poured into the labor force, where they typically work for lower wages than firms would have to pay male replacements.

Nostalgia Does Not Provide Guidance

If it is unlikely that we can return to the heyday of the breadwinner-homemaker family, or if it is simply unfair to make that our goal, then Gill's positions on divorce and employed mothers are of little help in formulating family policy. Enticing, coaxing, shaming, and even impoverishing women into staying married and staying home seems to make up virtually the entire conservative program. There is no vision of the future, just nostalgia for the past. Any measure that could remotely increase mothers' economic independence is opposed, no matter how many children it would help. Little thought is given to how men might increase their contribution to their children's well-being. Granted, the conservative lament for a lost era stems from a deep concern for children. But if we won't be returning to the 1950s anytime soon, then conservative writings about the family provide us with little guidance about where to go from here.

The Harmful Effects of Divorce Can Be Mitigated

by Richard Weissbourd

About the author: *Richard Weissbourd is a psychologist and a fellow at Harvard University's Kennedy School of Government.*

Editor's note: The names of the characters in this article have been changed.

When Fred Louis looks back at everything that went haywire in 1993—leaving school, drinking heavily, feeling bottomless misery—it seems as if his parents' divorce a decade before was at the root. An earnest, barrel-chested 17-year-old with a broad, mild smile, he didn't understand the full extent of the damage at first. In fact, he thought he had come to a kind of truce with the divorce. Instead, his feelings about the divorce sneaked up and uncoiled on him.

Divorce is often held responsible for the difficulties of millions of children like Fred. Divorce and unwed motherhood are being blamed for children's school troubles, delinquency, and drug abuse, as well as a renewed cycle of teenage pregnancy and family collapse. Yet the reality is far more complex than the cartoon.

Sarah and Bill Louis divorced when Fred, their second of three children, was seven years old. All Fred recalls prior to the divorce is his parents' "fighting about everything." Although Bill Louis had been attentive to Fred early in his childhood, in the year before the divorce Bill was home only on weekends. Though he was pleasant with Fred, he seemed in another world, glued to the television or tinkering endlessly with his sports car.

Although Fred was aware of trouble in his parents' marriage, the divorce blindsided him. One day his parents were together, it seemed, and the next day they were divorced. His older sister told him she had overheard a telephone conversation between their parents. Their father was not coming home again.

In fact, the marriage had begun to collapse about three years earlier. Sarah worked as a secretary for Bill's insulation business out of their home—and she

From Richard Weissbourd, "Divided Families, Whole Children." ©1994, New Prospect, Inc. Reprinted by permission from the *American Prospect*, Summer 1994.

recalls his carping at her constantly: "I didn't talk right, I wore the wrong clothes." In the last year of the marriage, Bill developed a serious alcohol problem. When he was drunk his anger spilled out viciously.

Sarah hated her marriage but felt emotionally and financially dependent on Bill. She was devastated when he told her that he had been seeing another woman and was moving in with her. Bill also insisted he needed their house for his business, and it was Sarah and the children who had to move out. Sarah landed a part-time nursing job, but she was still unable to adequately clothe and feed the three children every day. Within a few months she found another job in the evening that kept the family out of poverty. She arranged to have a neighbor watch all three of the children.

> *"Divorce is often held responsible for the difficulties of millions of children. . . . Yet the reality is far more complex than the cartoon."*

Hidden Pain

Sarah thinks that Fred, of all her children, took the divorce the hardest, though at first the damage was not apparent to her either. In fact, she leaned on Fred more than the other children after the divorce. By her lights, Fred had always maintained an inner sturdiness. He became a kind of partner to her, even though he was only seven years old. When she was upset, she depended on him to help with housework and to supervise his younger brother.

Fred, for his part, worried about his mother intensely. For hours, he recalls, she cried or stared blankly at the television. She looked like a zombie. Often he tried to buoy her, reassuring her that the pain would pass. And he hid from her how abandoned he felt by his father.

His mother, Fred recalls, pulled out of her fog about two years later, and for a few years life at home seemed easier and more pleasant than Fred had ever remembered. Around the time that Fred turned 11, however, his anger at his father, which had often gusted, turned into a gale. He saw his father about once a month, but his father—wearing black leather jackets, driving a motorcycle, racing professional drag cars—seemed pathetic, ashamed of his age. Bill Louis had also married the woman with whom he had been having the affair. She was a much younger woman; Fred felt she treated him like an interloper. Even more galling, Fred was told by his mother when he was 12 that his father was not paying child support.

When Fred started to become "cynical" in the ninth grade, it was his disillusionment with his father, he now believes, that was the source. He became a leader of the "druggie" gang, and fought frequently with rival gangs, though he was not a drug user himself. Although he managed to leave the gang, when he entered high school he lost contact with his father completely—"we just stopped calling each other"—and he found himself rudderless. The school seemed huge and impersonal. Not a single school administrator even knew his name. While he had been a leader in middle school, he was now "at the bottom of the totem pole." Nor could he turn to his mother for help. It seemed to him that Sarah was hardly ever home; when she was home she was distracted or critical of him.

Every day it now seemed to him that he was "rotting," that "the sand was going in the hourglass." School seemed almost surreal: "I was there but I couldn't figure out what I was supposed to do."

He began skipping school, sometimes persuading friends to skip with him. Sarah was shocked when she received the call from the assistant principal at Fred's school; Fred had been absent for 30 days. This was not, to be sure, the first time Fred had had school troubles: many times she had tried to persuade teachers to "look past the exterior," that beneath Fred's fighting with other children and sullen defiance was a bright child who simply needed some adult attention. But Sarah had always assumed that Fred, the child she relied on so completely, was suffering the normal downturns of adolescence. She recalls one reason she failed to notice the signs of Fred's distress: she was too consumed with his younger brother, Kim, who had recently been arrested for drug possession.

One night Fred came home drunk and erased any illusions his mother had about his taking the divorce in stride. All his troubles, he told her, stemmed from the divorce. Brimming with bitterness and disgust, he said

> *"Large numbers of children are spared serious problems because of divorce."*

that his father had betrayed him and the whole family. Not only had his father broken off contact with him, the man had ended up living quite comfortably, while the rest of the family had been dumped into poverty. The divorce, Fred said, had ruined it for all of them.

Divorce Is Not a Scourge

There is no question that divorce does harm to large numbers of children—Fred Louis is no exception. It is simply a myth that divorce doesn't damage kids. Yet it is also a myth that divorce is some modern scourge. Divorce and single parenthood are not the prime cause of school problems and other childhood problems in this country—and large numbers of children are spared serious problems because of divorce.

Divorce typically has complex costs and benefits for individual children like Fred. He was vulnerable in different ways after the divorce than he would have been had his parents' miserable marriage stayed intact. Fred felt ashamed and abandoned by his father after the divorce. But he may have felt ashamed and abandoned in different ways if the marriage had remained intact, with his father remote and constantly fighting with his mother. And while divorce brought many hardships to Sarah, it also pulled her out of a dead-end marriage that was

91

killing her spirit and badly compromising her ability to parent—and of course it was primarily upon her parenting, not Bill's, that Fred relied.

Further, the damage that divorce does to children varies enormously, depending on many factors such as the responsiveness of parents, schools, and community adults. Ideological warfare over the precise damage done by divorce is the wrong debate. Rather, policymakers and those who deal directly with children need a greater understanding of these complexities so that they can create communities and schools that will both help families stay together and keep children from unraveling when their families are torn apart.

The Impact of Divorce on Children

One serious consequence of divorce is that most children like Fred Louis will effectively lose their fathers. In some 90 percent of divorces, mothers are awarded custody of their children. Ten years after a divorce, fathers will be entirely absent from the lives of almost two-thirds of these children. Vanishing fathers often mean vanishing income—children are about twice as likely to be living in poverty after their parents divorce.

Those who decry divorce typically depict couples leaving each other casually and selfishly, out of boredom or a lack of fulfillment. They conjure up couples in the throes of mid-life crises itching to fulfill vague, immature ambitions or indulging themselves with younger lovers—a description that indeed fits Bill Louis. At the same time, few advocates of tougher divorce laws think women should stay with alcoholic and abusive husbands like Bill. Family therapists suggest that while some people divorce casually, people typically divorce for diverse and serious reasons, especially when children are involved. Often parents divorce because one or both partners are too immature to communicate effectively and to work through the inevitable disappointments and compromises of marriage. Sometimes a marriage cannot withstand the long illness or the long depression of a partner. Families can decay in many ways.

And children can suffer from many different kinds of family decay. Although statistics show that children from divorced families have more school and peer problems than children from intact families, they do not account for how children from divorced families would have fared had their parents not divorced but stayed together in rotting marriages. In fact, there is evidence that many children show signs of greater trouble in school months and even years prior to a divorce.

> *"Many children show signs of greater trouble in school months and even years prior to a divorce."*

A study that tracked children in a Berkeley (California) nursery school beginning in 1968 shows that years before their parents' split, boys whose parents would eventually divorce were more likely to exhibit various behavior problems, such as impulsiveness and rudeness, than boys whose families stayed together (far smaller differences were found among girls). Children in high-conflict homes are also just as likely to drop out of school, marry as teens, have a child before marrying, and themselves divorce as are children from divorced homes, according to researchers James Peterson and Nicholas Zill. While divorce appears to be one factor contributing to school problems, marriage problems, and work problems, it is by no means their primary cause.

Different Vulnerabilities

Consider Ann Waters, a lithe 10-year-old child in Boston. While many children like Fred end up in caretaking roles after divorce, Ann spent a good time taking care of her father *prior* to her parents' divorce. The father worked part-time and spent much of the day languishing around the house, often drunk and depressed. Ann's mother worked long hours, and every morning Ann awoke early to cook her father's breakfast. She also rushed home to run errands for him after school and to cook dinner. She enjoyed taking on these tasks, but her friendships suffered. Even when there was time Ann often felt like she was "too mature" for her friends. Her friends called her "bossy." In her free time she chose to read instead.

> *"While divorce appears to be one factor contributing to school problems, marriage problems, and work problems, it is by no means their primary cause."*

After the divorce, Ann was referred to a therapist by her mother, who said she was having temper tantrums. As her therapist puts it, after the divorce Ann suffered a kind of "demotion in the family." With her father out of the house, she no longer was a needed caretaker. Her mother was home more often but would not allow Ann to play this caretaker role. "Instead of treating Ann like an adult," this therapist adds, "Ann's mother treated her like she should treat her—as a ten year old—but Ann hated that. She became enraged about being treated like a child."

While Ann Waters was in turmoil after her parents' divorce, it is hard to argue that she was either better or worse off. She was simply vulnerable in different ways. Prior to the divorce, Ann was vulnerable because she shouldered responsibility for her father—a role that not only made it hard for her to make friends, but that made it hard for her to be a child. Had this marriage remained intact, these problems might have greatly intensified as Ann reached adolescence and sought some separation from her father. On the other hand, Ann's relationship with her father was certainly not wholly negative: the divorce deprived her of the consistent contact of a parent whom she loved and who loved her and who provided her with the satisfaction of being needed.

For many children divorce is not a single event but a series of events: their families will change shape several times and each arrangement strengthens them in certain ways and creates new vulnerabilities. Often children endure their parents' separation and divorce, life with a mother and her lover, and a re-marriage—75 percent of custodial mothers and 80 percent of fathers remarry. Remarriage often brings a new set of siblings and sometimes another divorce—the divorce rate is higher in second marriages than in first marriages. Their children's most important relationships are thus rearranged several times. Moreover, many of the variables that most strongly influence the fate of children of divorce—whether a father disappears, whether a remarriage occurs, the success and nature of the remarriage—are simply not variables that shape children's lives in intact families. According to David Kantor, a pioneering family therapist, "We need to create entirely different models for understanding children in intact families and in divorced families."

Important Factors in Divorce

It is not divorce per se that does lasting damage to children as much as the way divorce interacts with many circumstances surrounding it. Children are not only affected by how their parents handle divorce—by unexplained acrimony, by being used as weapons or as messengers in divorce wars, by how parents adjust to being alone—but also by their experiences in the larger world with friends, with community adults, and with school.

Often divorce is damaging to children like Fred Louis, for example, because it forces their families to move, wrenching them from old friends and familiar schools and communities and exposing them to poorer, often more dangerous neighborhoods. Studies cited by sociologist Stephanie Coontz disentangled the effects of divorce from the effects of moving to a new neighborhood after a divorce. Coontz found that dislocation was more likely to hurt children's school prospects than divorce per se. Even when children do not actually move, divorce can untether them from supporters and loved ones, such as their father's family and friends.

Schools figure powerfully in these dynamics. Social worker and divorce-researcher Dan Hertzel says that the damage done by divorce is often much deeper because school staff don't know how to talk to children about it (many typically elect not to talk about it at all), exacerbating the shame children often feel. Many children, Hertzel points out, will provoke or "test" their teachers after a divorce. "They want to know if teachers, too, will abandon them, and sometimes they may secretly hope that causing trouble will get their parents to come to a meeting together." Yet teachers have little or no training in how to respond to this testing.

> *"[Stephanie] Coontz found that dislocation was more likely to hurt children's school prospects than divorce per se."*

Hertzel adds that teachers are far more comfortable talking to children who have suffered the deaths of family members than they are to children who have suffered their parents' divorce: "There are no rituals for school staff that can guide them in dealing with children after a divorce." Schools also have few guidelines when faced with decisions about whether to maintain the involvement of fathers, whether to encourage divorced parents to make educational decisions for their children jointly, and whether to include stepparents or cohabitating adults in school activities. Often high turnover among teachers and other personnel, especially day-care workers, further compounds the damage done by divorce.

Most often, it is a chain of interactions involving children's attributes, parents' characteristics and the characteristics of schools and communities that determine the damage wrought by divorce. Fred Louis is endangered not only because he is abandoned by his father at a critical developmental stage, but because he loses contact with his father just as he is entering a large, impersonal high school where he has little close contact with adults, where he feels on the bottom of the totem pole and where many of his friends are similarly disaffected. Fred is also imperiled because he is thrust into a caretaker role prematurely and learns to cope with stress by asserting his independence and taking control—a coping strategy that is useful for him for a few years after the divorce but that may make it easy for him to slip into a leadership role in a gang and that may play a part in his escalating conflicts with teachers. At the same time, his mother, strapped by two jobs and preoccupied with his younger brother, does not know about his drift and is not contacted by the school for a month. Fred is endangered by a chain of interactions involving the loss of his father, his developmental stage, his specific coping strategies, his mother's coping strategies, his brother's troubles, a transition to high school, peers who are similarly distressed and an unresponsive school bureaucracy.

> *"Children from single parent homes, if supported by community . . . networks, are no more likely to drop out of school than children from intact families."*

Using Schools and Communities

Protecting kids from the problems of divorce surely requires providing families with the support and counseling they need to stay together, emphasizing the serious troubles that divorce can bring, and reminding parents, again and again, about their moral obligations to each other and their children. But it also requires creating communities and schools that give both parents and children in single parent families the steady support and responsiveness they need. Education researcher James Coleman has shown that children from single parent homes, if supported by community, educational, and religious networks, are no more likely to drop out of school than children from intact families. Yet the the nation's major economic and social institutions are not designed to support single parent families: they have not caught up with the realities of modern family life.

Helping children through the experience of divorce does not mean re-creating tight-knit neighborhoods: it does mean providing children and parents with a variety of opportunities for ongoing support. Community and school strategies that help children manage divorce should have at least four elements. They will help children maintain strong ties to both other children and adults. They will strengthen parents and help parents create lasting ties to other parents. They will engage fathers in children's lives. And they will furnish both children and parents opportunities to talk about and make sense of the experience of divorce.

Anchors in Children's Lives

Given that children from divorced families are likely to tumble through various family arrangements, it is hard to exaggerate the importance of anchors in their lives—children and adults outside of their families who are caring and attentive over time. Some communities and schools are now seeking to both deepen and extend children's involvement with other children and adults.

For example, many large high schools across the country are creating more personal environments within schools—environments where children spend the bulk of their day with the same group of teachers and students—by clustering teachers and students, for example, or by creating schools within schools or "houses" within schools. Multigrade classrooms—classrooms where children stay with the same teacher for two or even three years—enable teachers to deepen their involvement with children. Some high schools now have "advisory" periods each day—a time where students are able to surface a wide array of concerns. Often the same teacher runs these advisory periods with the same group of students all four years of high school. Reducing teacher turnover and turnover among day care providers—difficult as these tasks may be—can similarly give children greater ballast and a deeper faith in the solidity of adults. Reducing class room size and recruiting volunteers who free up teachers' time can heighten teachers' responsiveness to individual children. Sometimes even a small amount of empathy and responsiveness can make a critical difference. Fred Louis skids out of school in part because he has no sustained connection to an adult at school.

Schools cannot support kids and parents alone: they need to work in tandem with a wide array of community organizations and services. Mentoring programs, for example, can be crucial sources of support and affirmation. Unfortunately, as Mark Freedman demonstrates in his book, *The Kindness of Strangers*, in most current mentoring programs relationships are short-lived; adults lose interest or are tied up by other demands, say, or adults or children move—an experience that can widen the cracks in a child's basic faith

> *"Schools . . . need to involve non-custodial fathers in their children's school activities."*

that mentoring is supposed to narrow. If mentoring programs are to be part of the solution and not part of the problem, they need to recruit adults who are able to make long-term commitments to children.

Strengthening Single Parents

Strengthening both custodial mothers and absent fathers encompasses many strategies, including improving both the quantity and quality of child care, creating part-time work opportunities and flexible hours and developing family-friendly management training. Currently, parent and family support programs are burgeoning across the country, many of which are linked to schools. They are also unburdening parents by providing various services—such as parent skills and job information classes—and by strengthening ties among parents. While these programs are promising, they remain scattered. City governments need to provide these supports through schools and other community institutions.

Children also need their fathers, and programs are helping fathers overcome the various inner and outer obstacles that drive them away from

> *"Groups for children in the midst of divorce . . . offer other useful opportunities for children to come to terms with non-traditional family arrangements."*

their children after a divorce. Here, too, the basic public institutions need to engage fathers. Schools, for example, need to involve non-custodial fathers in their children's school activities. Extending the school day and offering evening activities at school will further expand opportunities for fathers to involve themselves in their children's education. Because so many children live with stepfathers or their mothers' partners, schools also need help in the complex task of determining how best to engage the various men who may be important to a child.

Because divorce is so deeply unfathomable to children, because it renders them so helpless, because they are so likely to feel rejected and disillusioned, it is critical that children have opportunities to talk to adults who are able to help make this experience comprehensible. As Hertzel points out, school staff need to be trained to develop rituals and non-intrusive ways of letting children know that the staff know a divorce has occurred and are available to talk about it. School staff also need to recognize when a child needs to talk to a counselor or social worker. Health care providers and many others who work with children need to be similarly sensitized to the problems of divorce and given rudimentary training in how to talk to kids about it. Groups for children in the midst of divorce and groups for children who are having difficulties with stepparents are cropping up in some schools and offer other useful opportunities for children to come to terms with non-traditional family arrangements. Because for many children, like Fred, the worst consequences of divorce are delayed, it is vital to create ongoing opportunities for children to make sense of the experience rather than only reaching out to children in the immediate wake of a divorce.

The happy irony is that many of the things that will help children after a divorce—such as supporting parents and including fathers in their children's education—will not encourage people to divorce; they will help families stay together. These various community supports thus serve two key aims of any sound family policy—keeping families together and keeping children in one piece when their families come apart.

Chapter 3

How Should Society Address the Issues of Divorce and Child Custody?

CURRENT CONTROVERSIES

Divorce and Child Custody: An Overview

by Susan Kellam

About the author: *Susan Kellam is a staff writer for the* CQ Researcher, *a weekly report on public policy issues.*

The tragedy of Marc and Zitta Friedlander began in the 1960s at Columbia University, where they met and fell in love while getting their doctorates in physics. They married and had two sons, but after 17 years, in 1986, they separated. The boys, ages 6 and 8, stayed with their mother, while the Maryland couple embarked on an increasingly bitter fight over final custody.

Not long after the breakup, Marc picked up his sons at school—without permission—and spirited them off to Atlanta, Ga. He brought them back two months later, and his regular visits with the boys resumed. But tensions were building.

One summer day in 1988, with the custody battle now two years old, Marc took the boys aside and showed them a semiautomatic pistol he had bought. A few days later, he shot his estranged wife several times in a parking lot at her office in McLean, Va. The next day, Marc was charged with murder.

To William P. Turner, a domestic relations master for the Montgomery County, Md., Circuit Court, the Friedlanders had seemed caring and deeply committed to their sons.

Nonetheless, Turner called the Friedlander case "a troublesome one." The children "had to endure the vindictiveness of both parents," he said. "They were caught in a taffy pull." Indeed Turner had learned of the gun, but because of all the previous squabbling, he had not been alarmed and did not notify the police.

The tragic incident fired off a warning to judicial systems around the country: Legal battles involving children must not be allowed to drag on for years. The concern is all the greater because skyrocketing illegitimacy and divorce rates are leaving an increasing number of children under the control of the courts.

In 1993, more than a quarter of all American children under 18—27 per-

From Susan Kellam, "Child Custody and Support," *CQ Researcher*, January 13, 1995. Reprinted with permission.

cent—lived with one parent, up from 12 percent in 1970. The majority live with their mothers, but an increasing proportion reside with dad—13 percent in 1993, up from 9 percent in 1970.

In trying to help embattled couples resolve custody problems, domestic court judges must deal with a wide range of new circumstances. In light of new "gender-neutral" laws, they must render decisions that favor neither mothers nor fathers, they must deal with the new realities of advanced reproductive technology, weighing the rights of the biological parent versus the adoptive parent; and they must com-

> *"Skyrocketing illegitimacy and divorce rates are leaving an increasing number of children under the control of the courts."*

pare the merits of the primary caretaker with those of the parent most able to care for the child financially.

Enforcement of support payments for the growing proportion of children living in one-parent homes is the flip side of the custody battle. Following a separation or divorce, the parent who doesn't have primary responsibility for the child's physical custody is generally required to make support payments. The Congressional Research Service estimates that only $13 billion of the $34 billion in outstanding support orders were collected in 1993.

Resolving Disputes

Soon after Zitta Friedlander's death, a Governor's Task Force on Family Law was convened in Maryland to scrutinize the systems overseeing divorce procedures, including determination of child support and child custody. A key recommendation in the final report, issued in 1992, called for divorce attorneys to inform all clients with children of "nonlitigating means of resolving the dispute, including mediation, family counseling, or other alternate means of dispute resolution."

Rita R. Rosenkrantz, another domestic relations master in Montgomery County, heeded the recommendation when she initiated a countywide pilot project in 1993 designed to identify divorce cases involving children and settle them quickly. "We were told that custody should be resolved more promptly, and we paid attention to that," she says. "Certainty is more important than waiting—it prevents child snatching."

Divorce mediation has become a common feature in many domestic-relations courts. The National Center for State Courts in Arlington, Va., estimates that more than 205 programs now offer dispute resolution services in divorces, including battles over custody, visitation and child support. In addition to these public services, there are thousands of private divorce mediators, plus training programs and membership associations for mediators.

However, family law attorneys and advocates for children say that mediation is not the panacea for an overburdened domestic legal system. "If one of the parents is emotionally stronger than the other, it could break down," says James L. Rider, a Washington attorney who has mediated custody battles. "I've stopped mediations, not because I couldn't get a deal—but because I didn't like the deal I got."

Changes in state laws that began two decades ago, giving equal rights to both parents in a divorce case, tended to make custody fights even more contentious. At one end of the spectrum are women's rights groups arguing that mothers, especially those who work, are now being held by the courts to a higher standard of parental care.

At the other end is the burgeoning fathers' rights movement, championing the importance of paternal contact and lobbying hard for more joint custody legislation. The first National Summit on Fatherhood was held October 27–28, 1994, in Dallas, Texas, with Vice President Al Gore delivering the opening remarks. "When was the last time you went to your child's school or met with their teacher?" he asked fathers. "And last, but certainly not least, especially if you are divorced, do you treat your child's mother with respect?"

> *"Divorce mediation has become a common feature in many domestic-relations courts."*

The questions being asked by federal and state officials with increasing urgency go straight to two key money issues: paternity establishment and child support. The basic responsibility for administering child support enforcement is left to the states, but since 1975 Congress has played a key role in funding their efforts and monitoring the success rate. More than $2.2 billion in federal and state funds was spent in 1994 by state child support enforcement offices to collect $9 billion and track down and establish paternity for 554,205 children. . . .

Meanwhile, there is growing debate among child advocates over whether the child support system should be turned over to the federal government, with key collection responsibility given to the Internal Revenue Service (IRS). "We've spent 25 years in a state-based system that doesn't work. Give it to the IRS," says Paula Roberts, a senior attorney with the Center for Law and Social Policy.

But Douglas Besharov, a resident scholar at the American Enterprise Institute (AEI), calls it "idiocy to think that the IRS [would be] effective." He concedes, however, that child support may very well be federalized "unless the Republicans come to their senses" because "they, like the Democrats, feel that if there's a problem there should be a federal solution."

As the courts, lawmakers and child welfare experts debate how best to handle child custody and support, [various issues are being debated].

Maternal Preference in Custody Decisions

Judge Raymond R. Cashen of the Macomb County Circuit Court in the Detroit suburbs touched off a furious controversy in July 1994 when he awarded custody to Steven Smith of his 3-year-old daughter Maranda. Cashen had been swayed by the fact that Maranda's mother, Jennifer Ireland, put her in a small day-care center while attending classes at the University of Michigan. Steven Smith was also going to school, but his mother offered to watch Maranda. In Cashen's eyes, that made Smith the better parent.

Similarly, many working moms felt the impact of another 1994 decision, by District of Columbia Superior Court Judge Harriet R. Taylor, awarding custody of two small boys to their father, Kenneth Greene. The mother, Sharon Prost, was allowed visitation and ordered to make $23,010 a year in child-support payments. Prost, legal counsel to Republicans on the Senate Judiciary Committee, had failed at "striking a delicate balance" between job and family, the judge ruled.

But these cases are most noteworthy because they are the exception—not the rule.

One of the major changes in domestic law during the past two decades has been to end the bias toward maternal preference in custody cases. Nonetheless, courts have had difficulty abandoning decades of legal reasoning to adopt a new approach to custody decisions, according to several recent studies.

In the late 1980s, social researchers Eleanor E. Maccoby and Robert H. Mnookin of Stanford University studied 933 California families as they made post-separation arrangements for their children. Of the 53 cases in which both parents sought sole custody, the mother won 45 percent of the time; the father, 11 percent. In more than a third of the contested cases, the outcome was joint physical custody.

The Favored Parent

A team of sociologists who examined custody decisions in Utah from 1970 to 1993 found similar results. After examining 1,087 divorce cases, they found that among couples in which custody was disputed, custody was awarded to the mother 50 percent of the time and to the father 21 percent of the time. The remaining 29 percent of the cases resulted in some form of shared custody.

Sonny Burmeister, president of the Georgia chapter of the Children's Rights Council, a Washington-based advocacy group for joint custody, recounts the words of a former superior court judge in Cobb County, Ga.: "I ain't never seen the calves follow the bull, they always follow the cow. Therefore, I always give custody to the mama."

> *"One of the major changes in domestic law . . . has been to end the bias toward maternal preference in custody cases."*

Other anecdotal data, however, suggest that when the father does challenge the mother for custody, he has a good shot at winning. Judges are supposed to take into account such factors as who has been the primary caretaker, what is in the best interests of the child, which parent will be most cooperative about visits from the other parent and who is better equipped financially.

Jessica Strickland, a family law attorney in Decatur, Ill., says that the roles are still quite clear in the Midwest. "Mom is generally the one that does all the nitty-gritty child care, puts them in the bath and goes to the grocery store," she says. Consequently, when the family breaks up, mom generally gets the children, Strickland says.

> *"Some experts in the field strongly believe that the maternal preference is a thing of the past—and lament its passing."*

Rosenkrantz admits that as a domestic relations master, she finds the choices she faces somewhat clouded. "Who has done most of the parenting is not as clear-cut as it used to be," she says. Indeed, she finds that fathers play so much more of a role that she no longer assumes that the mother is the more nurturing parent. As a former colleague recently told Rosenkrantz: "Rita, you're harder on women."

Attorney Rider, who has won custody cases for both men and women, often urges judges not to hold women to a higher custodial standard. He observes that "judges, mostly those who are 50 or older, have preconceived ideas of the mom and dad roles. When the dad does 30 percent of the work with the children, the mom [is seen as not having] quite fulfilled her job at 70 percent. When the dad does 40 percent, you get a dead heat in a custody battle."

AEI's Besharov argues that "the custody cases that go to court are the ones that are too close to call. The lawyers [for men] know what they're doing and know they have a 50-50 chance of winning."

The Effects of Gender-Neutral Laws

Some experts in the field strongly believe that the maternal preference is a thing of the past—and lament its passing. Mary Ann Mason, a professor of law and social welfare at the University of California-Berkeley, puts much of the blame on gender-neutral laws, which say decisions should be made in the best interests of a child of divorce. Such laws create "confusion and manipulation on the part of fathers who intimidate mothers by threatening to go for custody if the woman asks for more child support," she says.

Nancy Erickson, an attorney with the New York–based National Center on Women and Family Law, says that "we're hearing reports from legal services attorneys across the country where the mother, or the state, sues for child support and the father turns around and sues for custody." More often than not, she says, the father wins custody because he is in a better financial situation than the mother.

"It's very grim, extremely grim," she says. "We're leaning in the direction of saying that when the office of child support brings a case against a father, then the government has to supply legal representation for the mother if her custody is challenged. They've gotten her into this pickle in the first place. Many of the mothers would be happy not to have money from the dad, it's not worth the trouble—for the few dollars they get."

Paula Roberts, of the Center for Law and Social Policy, is concerned about the mothers on the verge of collapse who work three jobs to support the children and then lose custody. That happens, she says, because courts tend to view the father—who often has not been paying child support—as more financially capable of providing support.

Citing the case of 3-year-old Maranda, Roberts points out that it was only after her mother asked for more child support that the father requested custody. "This is when the courts should stand up and say no to the dad," she says.

Wade F. Horn, director of the National Fatherhood Initiative, an advocacy group founded in 1993 and headquartered in Lancaster, Pa., agrees that the removal of maternal preference has had unintended consequences. "It's terrible," says Horn, a child psychologist. "But those cases are still the exception, not the rule. Certainly they are not a victory for men. They continue a [trend] that's not good for kids. What we want the courts to be saying is, 'You as the mother and you as the father should both be involved.'"

Joint Custody

The removal of the maternal preference standard paved the way for the emergence of a new custody arrangement. In 1979, the first joint custody statute was enacted in California, followed by Kansas and Oregon. Currently, 43 states have statutes that advocate joint custody as either an option or a preference; no state bars the arrangement. Proponents say joint custody gives children the care and affection they need from both parents and eliminates the burden of single parenting. Opponents argue that it robs children of a stable family environment, exacerbates parental conflict and in some cases gives violent spouses continuing control over the family.

There are two basic types of joint custody. Under joint *physical* custody, parents share their time with the children as equally as possible. Joint *legal* custody, on the other hand, gives parents equal input in all decisions affecting the children, such as choosing medical treatment and schools.

> *"One of the ongoing debates is whether joint custody should be ordered when one or both parents are opposed to the arrangement."*

An extensive study of different types of custody conducted at the Center for Policy Research in Denver, Colo., found that conflict between parents did not worsen as a result of the increased communication through shared parenting. It was the parents with sole maternal physical custody who reported the greatest deterioration in the relationships over time. On the other hand, according to sociologists Jessica Pearson and Nancy Thoennes, parents attracted to a joint physical custody arrangement are "predisposed to cooperate and do not suffer from the higher levels of family violence observed in sole custody situations."

One of the ongoing debates is whether joint custody should be ordered when one or both parents are opposed to the arrangement. Numerous attorneys contend that it only works with two parents keen about the concept. Others maintain that many divorcing parents know little about the arrangement initially but grow to appreciate the benefits with experience.

Custody Battles in High-Conflict Families

Maccoby and Mnookin were alarmed by the results of their California study showing that joint physical custody decrees are frequently used to try to resolve disputes in high-conflict families. Of the 166 cases resulting in joint custody, 36 percent involved substantial or intense legal conflict. They also noted that in about half of the high-conflict cases, the umbrella term of joint custody was misleading because the children actually lived with the mother.

Pearson concurs, noting that her research indicates that joint residential custody is rare, often less than 5 percent of custody decisions in many jurisdictions. She attributes the decrease in the use of shared custody to the financial difficulty of maintaining two households that can accommodate the children.

"The trend toward joint residential custody is over."

The trend toward joint residential custody is over, agrees Neal J. Meiselman, a Rockville, Md., attorney. "It's an anti-trend. I've sat in settlement conferences and seen judges who won't grant joint custody unless the parents get along," he says.

Many observers viewed a change in California's joint custody law in 1989 as a sign that splitting the child's time may not be the ideal solution to a disintegrating family. The change was made in the state's 10-year-old joint custody law after women's rights groups successfully lobbied for an amendment explicitly stating that there is no preference for joint custody unless both parents request it.

Ronald Henry, a pro bono attorney for the Children's Rights Council in Washington and a joint custody advocate, argues that "political advocacy has gotten in the way of good science. Mothers' groups are trying to tar joint custody by comparing it to an intact marriage." The more apt comparison, he says, is with sole custody, which reduces the father's role.

"I like joint custody because it makes a statement that both parents are vital to the process," adds Rider. "It really means that they have equal decision-making powers."

But, Rider cautions, there are drawbacks. "I've seen situations where the dad has used his legal decision-making authority as a veto power," he says. He recalls a young girl who was prevented from traveling with the cast of a major show because the father asserted his "no" vote.

"Sole custody is even worse," counters Burmeister of the Georgia Children's Rights Council. "The parent with total control and authority can really use it against the other parent."

Illinois lawyer Strickland calls joint custody "an absolutely meaningless phrase until parents sit down and iron out the details. Most divorcing people are not that friendly. It's a rare solution because we still have to have someone who runs the kids to the doctors. It was a sound-good thing—that's why legislators passed the laws."

Mason, who also maintains that joint custody only works when parents are in close cooperation, has been deluged by divorcing parents since the publication of her book, *From Father's Property to Children's Rights: The History of Child Custody in the United States.*

"Literally dozens of mothers called me who felt they were being intimidated by husbands threatening them with joint custody," she says. "I've gotten hate letters from angry fathers saying I was being unfair to men." Clearly, she says, the custody debate is very much alive.

Divorce Laws Should Be Reformed

by Robert L. Plunkett

About the author: *Robert L. Plunkett is the vice dean of the Southern California Institute of Law and a professor at the University of La Verne School of Law in La Verne, California.*

Much has been written in the last twenty years about the state of marriage. These commentaries tend to fall into two opposite camps: those which advocate or celebrate the redefinition of matrimony and those which deplore its decline. Two decades ago, the former clearly predominated; the latter are more common today. To my knowledge, however, none of the commentators has stumbled upon the fact that marriage was abolished in the United States in the 1970s. That status which we call "being married" today is nothing of the kind; it is to real marriage what the Holy Roman Empire was to the real Roman Empire, something that borrows the name of a dead institution to give itself legitimacy.

According to *Black's Law Dictionary*, in marriage "a man and woman . . . mutually engage with each other to live their whole lives together in the state of union which ought to exist between a husband and wife." That quotation summarizes definitions set forth by precedents and authorities going as far back as such things are preserved. In simple terms, the essentials of a marriage are: 1) a man and woman 2) in a state of union 3) for life. There are variations from time to time and from society to society. In polygamous cultures, for instance, one man can have many marriages, but each is a one-man-and-one-woman contract.

The "for life" part of the definition has been more or less elastic since at least Roman times. But the promise to be married "until death do you part" was, until the establishment of no-fault divorce, binding on at least one of the parties as long as the other remained blameless. Where women were chattel, the wedding vow was breakable by the husband but unbreakable by the wife. Where a tribeswoman could turn out her husband at will, the husband was bound to stay with the wife until she either threw him out or did something wrong that would justify his leaving.

It was established long ago by the courts that alleged marriage vows which did not contemplate a lifetime union did not create a marriage. Saying "I promise to be your wife for five years" did not make someone a wife for even one second. With even stronger logic, a vow to be husband and wife "as long as we want" was no marriage vow. A purported marriage ceremony established a marriage if and only if at least one of the participants believed that they were making a commitment to which they would be held for life.

What is this thing we currently call "marriage"? Most wedding ceremonies still contain the requisite language about "forsaking all others," remaining together "for richer for poorer, in sickness and in health, until death do you part." But these words have no basis in reality. Under current law the bride and groom are in fact promising to be husband and wife only until one of them doesn't want to any more. The lifetime commitment which defined marriage is gone.

"You can't stop somebody from getting a divorce if they really want one." That is the first thing an ethical lawyer today tells someone who is trying to avoid a divorce. Divorce for the asking is the rule. Even if a state required more, that could easily be gotten around by establishing a brief residence in a state that wasn't so picky.

The History of Divorce

In 1969, when California Governor Ronald Reagan signed the nation's first no-fault divorce law, he and the legislature talked as if they were merely reforming the existing system by establishing a single humane standard for the dissolution of marriage. Supposedly, they were simply making it easier for those trapped in hopeless unions to fix their lives by getting out. It was hailed as a progressive reform and quickly imitated by almost every other state. It was a noncontroversial act, buried in the news by the Vietnam War and other concerns. Yet signing the no-fault divorce law may have been the most important thing Reagan did in his entire political career. To understand why, we need to review the history of divorce.

Anglo-American jurisprudence once considered marriage a sacrament, or at least an unbreakable vow. While a marriage might be annulled in circumstances which struck at its validity, such as concealed impotence, a marriage, once valid, was set in stone. This was true even if both spouses desperately wanted a divorce, because in making their marriage vows they were deemed to have made a covenant not only with each other but also with God and society. As late as 1900, fewer than one thousand divorces a year were granted in all of Britain.

> *"The lifetime commitment which defined marriage is gone."*

The iron rule against divorce softened with the adoption of the principle that a person who was grievously wronged by his or her spouse should get relief from the courts and that this relief could include the right to get out of the marriage. When people "sued for divorce," they actually were filing a suit against the other spouse, just as if they were suing for personal injury or breach of contract. To get a divorce, the petitioner had to show that the respondent was guilty. If guilt was found, there would usually be not only a divorce but damages in the form of alimony and loss of property.

The grounds for divorce, primarily adultery and desertion, were originally narrow and directly related to the marriage contract. Furthermore, divorce was granted only when an innocent party sued a guilty one. If, for instance, the wife and the husband each proved that the other had committed adultery, the couple had to stay married, because the guilt of one spouse canceled out the guilt of the other. If you watch old movies, you might hear a character say, "My wife won't give me a divorce." This meant that the wife wouldn't go along with his seeking a divorce and that she refused to seek one herself based on whatever grounds she had. Under the fault divorce system, the innocent spouse had an absolute right to keep the marriage together.

The idea of divorce as a lawsuit by a good spouse against a bad one eroded over the decades as a result of misuse and the "reform" it encouraged. There were two major types of misuse. First, one party let the other trump up a phony adultery or desertion purely to meet the letter of the law. Second, courts stretched the letter of the law to absurd lengths to accommodate the parties—for example, by ruling that trivial incidents qualified as "extreme mental cruelty." But this worked only if the husband and wife were in cahoots.

> *"Had the first no-fault divorce law been presented as one that would allow either spouse to dissolve the marriage at his or her whim, it almost certainly would have been defeated."*

The misuse of existing divorce law involved blatant hypocrisy and frequent perjury, but it did not strike at the essence of marriage as a lifetime commitment. So-called reform of the divorce laws, inspired largely by distaste for collusive divorce, did far more damage. By creating new grounds such as "incompatibility," legislators sought to get away from the idea that you could end a marriage only if one spouse was bad and the other good. These attempts to graft a nonfault ground onto the traditional system of suing for divorce led to some odd legal decisions. Then came the idea of no-fault divorce.

The Abolition of Marriage

By 1970, among the intelligentsia, the idea that marriage was a sacred commitment was as dead as Queen Victoria, and the idea that marriages should be preserved for some reason independent of the happiness of the couple was comatose. The belief that people should not be forced to stay in bad marriages was firmly established among our policy- and opinion-makers. No-fault divorce fit this new dogma perfectly. Instead of inquiring into whether the husband or wife was bad, the courts would inquire into whether the marriage was bad. Instead of suing for divorce, one would petition to dissolve the marriage. Issues of fault and blame would be eliminated.

> *"The wedding vow [has] devolved from being the most serious and solemn oath a typical person ever [makes] into being less than a contract."*

Had the first no-fault divorce law been presented as one that would allow either spouse to dissolve the marriage at his or her whim, it almost certainly would have been defeated. It appears that everybody whose opinion counted believed that its sole effect would be to make it easier to end hopeless marriages. After all, the law's main innovation was to allow the dissolution of marriages afflicted with "irreconcilable differences which have led to the irremediable breakdown of the marriage." Few, given the dominant ideology of the time, could oppose divorce in that situation.

The people who believed that the law would be applied to end only truly hopeless marriages were incredibly naïve. The courts were ill equipped and ill disposed to inquire into whether differences were "irreconcilable" or whether a marriage had suffered an "irremediable" breakdown. In fact, the mere filing of a petition for dissolution of marriage was deemed sufficient. The inquiry into whether the grounds for dissolution existed was in practice limited to the petitioning party's reciting of the statutory language verbatim or checking a box on a form, which did the same thing. It was divorce for the asking, pure and simple.

This was the abolition of marriage. Whatever words were used in the ceremony, weddings ceased to be occasions where a man and woman mutually engaged to live their whole lives together as husband and wife. They became occasions where a man and woman agreed to call themselves husband and wife until one of them decided otherwise. In the late Sixties, some intellectuals advocated "trial marriages," in which people would try each other out before committing to real marriage. This talk faded as it sank in that *every* marriage was now a trial marriage.

No Penalties

The wedding vow had devolved from being the most serious and solemn oath a typical person ever made into being less than a contract. An oral contract made with a 2-year-old is more binding than the contract of marriage; it at least binds one party, the adult. A marriage contract is binding on no one. If Kim Basinger says "OK" when asked by a producer if she will star in a movie and then backs out, she has made herself liable for millions of dollars in damages. If she solemnly swears in church to love, honor, and, forsaking all others, keep only unto that producer till death them do part, she is free to break that promise at any time without penalty.

Many people who have gone through divorce or seen others do so will object to the phrase "without penalty." They know the dissolution of marriage carries with it great potential expense and financial loss. There's the division of property, child support, and possibly even spousal support.

Those may seem like penalties, but they are not. For one thing, they represent nothing more than the state's effort to dissolve the marital partnership equitably. A divorcing man may lose his house, but it is not as a penalty; it is because the house was only half his all along. Child support is only the discharge of the continuing obligation of supporting one's child, an obligation that would have existed even if there had never been a marriage. Spousal support is a safety net for a spouse who was out of the labor force.

More to the point, these things are not penalties because they fall equally hard on the guilty and the innocent. The spouse who broke the promise to live together as husband and wife is on an equal legal footing with the spouse who followed it faithfully. The fact that one spouse broke his or her marriage vows has no bearing on his or her rights to property, support, etc. No-fault means no distinction between the victim and the wrongdoer.

Couples go into marriage today figuring that if they don't like it they can always get a divorce. Though some still talk as if they are definitely in it for life, it is disturbing how many say things *at their weddings* like, "We'll see how long it lasts." People who talk as if their marriages are for life usually are greeted with comments like, "You might be one of the lucky ones," spoken in tones ranging from openly skeptical to patronizing.

More Blows Against Marriage

Almost at the same time that the wedding vow was stripped of its essential meaning, the whole idea of marriage as a special estate was also being undermined from several other directions. "Palimony," the right of a nonmarital partner to seek marriage-like financial rights based on an express or implied contract, blurred the distinction between marriage and what was once called "living in sin." Another blow against marriage was the repeal of virtually all laws against adultery, cohabitation, and fornication, as well as all laws making a distinction between legitimate and illegitimate parenthood. This development was accompanied by the elimination of the stigma connected with all of these. These changes destroyed all real distinction between having sex or children in wedlock and having them extramaritally.

> *"Couples go into marriage today figuring that if they don't like it they can always get a divorce."*

The idea that divorce should carry a stigma is moribund. In fact, divorce is more often applauded than deplored. When one of the two most popular advice columnists in the country ended her marriage after decades of telling others to stick it out, rather than outcry about her hypocrisy, there was much commentary about how this showed her "growth." The existence of commercial divorce congratulation cards shows how something which was once a subject of shame has become a cause for celebration for many.

About all that is left separating the wed from the unwed is the illusion that marriage still exists in a meaningful way and a dwindling list of benefits that are still reserved for married couples, such as family health-care insurance and joint tax filing. Even these are under attack, not by people who want to take them away from married couples but by people who want them to apply to non-marital partners. These proposals have so much support because so-called marriage has deteriorated into a removable label, a ticket to certain perks.

For the Sake of the Children?

Between the time that the belief that marriage was sacred fell out of fashion and the time that the thinking behind no-fault divorce took hold, the chief argument for keeping unhappy marriages intact was for the sake of the children. The term "broken home" was applied to a family that was missing a parent because of divorce; it was a sad word used for a situation that was universally deemed to be unfortunate.

Around the time that no-fault divorce was created, the term "broken home" fell out of use and was replaced by a plethora of happy euphemisms. In place of the old ideas about the importance of intact families were new ones about how a stable, traditional family structure was either unimportant or actually harmful to kids. The notions which supported the dogma that children could thrive in what had once been called broken homes ranged from the plausible but wrong, like the idea that stepparents could fully replace birth

> *"Four years after the adoption of the first no-fault divorce law, divorce passed death as the leading cause of family breakup."*

parents, to the plainly idiotic, such as the claim that children were better off when released from an unhappy marriage. The latter ignored the fact that unhappy marriages are unhappy for the parents, and the happiness of the parents is rightly less important to children than having both of their parents around.

After a generation of experimentation with single-parent families and all manner of stepdads, moms' boyfriends, and such, the results are in. Children from single-parent families are more than five times as likely to live in poverty, nearly twice as likely to need psychological help, and two and a half times as likely to drop out of school, get pregnant before marriage, abuse drugs, and commit crimes as are children from intact families.

Half of all marriages end in divorce. Four years after the adoption of the first no-fault divorce law, divorce passed death as the leading cause of family breakup. Every year more than a million children go through divorce and separation.

People who deplore the effects of single-parent upbringing focus on the booming rate of illegitimacy, all but ignoring the other half of the problem, the catastrophic divorce rate. In fact, the silence on the latter issue seems largely based on an unspoken assumption that divorce is like a force of nature, beyond human control.

Similarly, commentators who wax eloquent about the ill effects of un-wed motherhood on teenaged mothers seem unaware of the ill effects of divorce on adults, especially women. The leading article on single-parent families, "Dan Quayle Was Right," by Barbara Dafoe Whitehead (1993),

> *"A husband or wife who faithfully performs his or her duties in the marriage should have the absolute right to insist that the marriage remain intact."*

treated divorce as a good thing for the parents even while making a convincing case for its ill effects on children. But the abolition of marriage has been a disaster for people of all ages.

No More Lifetime Commitment

People earnestly want commitment from their beloved, but it is no longer possible to have final commitment to or from anybody. You can devote your life to someone else, but the law and society give you no security against the other person's leaving and making all your effort pointless. People are rational; when they know this they will, for their own protection, hold back on giving love and making sacrifices. Knowing that they can be thrown away at any time and that divorce has become the rule rather than the exception has transformed married couples from partners in life's journey into players in a game of prisoner's dilemma.

When divorce was available only to a wronged party, a wife could see her husband through his hard times knowing that she could hold onto him through hers. A woman at the peak of her attractiveness could work full time while her husband went through medical school, knowing that he could not easily leave her when he was rich and she middle-aged. Now, he can take her at her best and leave her whenever a better offer comes along. So we have legions of discarded older ex-wives of now successful men.

There is nothing inevitable or immutable about the abolition of marriage. The divorce rate can be brought under control by mere mortals. Make it harder to leave a marriage, and more people will decide they can make a go of it after all.

Marriages should be dissolvable only by mutual agreement or on grounds, such as adultery, desertion, and criminal physical abuse, that clearly involve a wrong by one party against the other and that by their very nature constitute a violation of the marriage vows as they are traditionally understood. A husband or wife who faithfully performs his or her duties in the marriage should have the absolute right to insist that the marriage remain intact. The addition of "mutual agreement" to the traditional grounds for divorce eliminates the need for fraudulent, collusive divorces by preserving the right of couples to end a marriage in which they both feel trapped.

To properly re-establish marriage, we should also abolish the Reno-style quickie divorce. Even before no-fault, the divorce laws were made a mockery, at least for the rich, by the ease with which one could shop around for a favorable divorce jurisdiction. When divorces were hard to get in most states, everyone knew they could be obtained easily in Nevada and a few other places. This meant that the restrictive laws of 49 states could be undone by one. Federal legislation should require that the law of the state where the wedding ceremony took place be controlling on the issue of whether any particular marriage could be dissolved.

Much of the social pathology, moral breakdown, alienation, and rootlessness that afflict our society today can be traced to the abolition of marriage. These will remain with us until their cause is effectively dealt with. Of course, the first step toward re-establishing marriage as an institution is to recognize that it was disestablished in the first place. The next step is to change the laws that abolished it.

Divorce Laws Should Not Be Reformed

by Martha Albertson Fineman

About the author: *Martha Albertson Fineman is Maurice T. Moore Professor of Law at Columbia University and author of* The Illusion of Equality: The Rhetoric and Reality of Divorce Reform.

Marriage stands condemned as a failed social institution in the eyes of many at the end of the 20th century. Increasingly, people are marrying later in life, while others choose not to marry at all. Meanwhile, the divorce rate hovers near 50 percent for all new marriages. Out-of-wedlock motherhood is on the rise, particularly among the well-educated, according to 1990 census data summarized by Amaru Bachu in the journal *Current Population Reports*. Furthermore, the historical assumption that the private, marital-based (or nuclear) family unit can comfortably accept primary responsibility for the care of children and other family members seems increasingly untenable. Marriage is not a realistic bedrock for social policy, although it seems a convenient panacea to politicians and pundits discussing the divorce rate, the shocking figures on child poverty or plans to promote so-called "family values." And if marriage as a social institution is failing, harsh and punitive measures designed to make the status more rigid and inflexible are absurd.

Policymakers are reluctant to see that a social phenomenon such as a high divorce rate is merely one component in a panoply of indicators chronicling the widespread and irrevocable nature of the changes that have occurred in all areas of our collective lives. We stand in the midst of significant social change and it is important that we realize that there is no uncomplicated past, no lingering utopian vision to which the law can return us.

Our societal goal should be to fashion rules that reflect the ways in which people are living their lives. We should subsidize and support the emerging family units, such as single-mother families, that are performing the valuable task of caring for children and other family members. Recognizing these units

From Martha Albertson Fineman, "Icon of Marriage Has Had Its Day," *Insight*, June 27, 1994.
Reprinted by permission of *Insight* magazine; ©1994 by News World Communications, Inc. All rights reserved.

as a social reality is not to deny that changing patterns of behavior have the potential for serious consequences, particularly for children. Our obsession with the idealized nuclear family, however, has meant that our solutions for real problems have not been practical or realistic, but reactionary paeans to distorted images of "days gone by."

There are significant moral issues associated with the failure of marriage—issues that the current focus of reviving the nuclear family has obscured. Important family issues do not revolve around the question of whether no-fault divorce laws are good or bad social policy. Today's family problems are access to medical care, housing, jobs and education in a society that fails to consider such elements basic human entitlements.

Divorce has exposed the vulnerability of children in our society, which would only be worsened by divorce-focused "reforms." Resurrecting obstacles to divorce simply reinforces the myth that the "private family" offers the best solutions for inevitable dependency and the poverty our current policies have generated. Indeed, the self-sufficient nuclear family, providing for all its members without making demands on the state, was never a reality—the family has always enjoyed legal and ideological subsidies through laws governing inheritance, bankruptcy, insurance and taxes.

A Collective Responsibility to Children

The romantic image of the nuclear family is an especially unrealistic one, given today's economy and the federal government's abandonment of social policies aimed at full employment and guarantees of a basic set of entitlements for all Americans. One need only look at the figures to know that marriage, or any basic social policy that relies primarily on private responsibility, will fail. One in five children lives in poverty. One in six has no medical insurance. Tens of thousands are homeless. At least one in four is feeling the effects of hunger, suffering from such problems as inadequate diet, malnutrition and chronic food shortages.

These statistics do not represent failures attributable to divorce or individual shortcomings. They are the casualties of a cultural revolution in the way American men and women relate to each other and the way society views collective responsibilities for children. They are a national disgrace, and it is about time we started viewing them as such and fashioning remedies that recognize that we have a collective responsibility to children.

> *"Important family issues do not revolve around the question of whether no-fault divorce laws are good or bad social policy."*

Americans frequently ignore basic human realities in favor of simplistic platitudes that pass as conventional wisdom. We cannot afford to continue to do this when the nation's children are at stake. We must confront the fact that dependency is inevitable—it is an inherent human condition that inescapably accompanies childhood and illness and often results from disability and advancing age. It is not only a private matter but a public responsibility as well. Divorce reform ignores this basic tenet and keeps us inappropriately focused on the failings of spouses.

Laws Must Reflect Societal Reality

We should remember that law is of limited usefulness as a device for transforming a society. Laws that fail to reflect the realities of the society in which they are forged are doomed to be ignored, violated or manipulated in accordance with dominant societal understandings of what is appropriate behavior. Furthermore, even if law were generally conceded to be an effective tool for change, it would take much more than just rescinding the divorce reforms and returning to a fault-based system to compel people to remain in lifelong monogamous relationships.

It is time for the legal system to abandon marriage as a defining characteristic of the family. In the end, marriage is only a legal category. Marriage does not enforce love, cooperation or harmonious and supportive cohabitation. Even an outright prohibition on divorce would not achieve much in terms of altering behavior—unless we bolstered it with other regulatory and intrusive laws.

When divorce was harder to obtain, abandonment was common. Therefore, in addition to reintroducing fault, the law would have to strengthen its punishment of desertion or abandonment and extramarital sexual relations. Without such complementary regulations, illegal sexual liaisons would offer a tempting alternative for those locked into a marriage they could not escape.

In the fault system, spouses who agreed to end their relationship frequently did so on fabricated grounds. So, if we stiffen the grounds for divorce by requiring that fault of one spouse be proved, we also would have to outlaw and punish connivance. And, of course, we would have to worry about increases in violence fueled by the desperation and frustration of those who perceived no alternative and no escape from a bad marriage.

> *"Even an outright prohibition on divorce would not achieve much in terms of altering behavior—unless we bolstered it with other regulatory and intrusive laws."*

If states restore the fault-based divorce rules, will they reinstitute complementary laws that also reflect society's preference for formal marriage as the only basis for legitimate sexual relationships? Are we willing to reinstate criminal sanctions against fornication, adultery, nonmarital cohabitation and other potentially marriage-threatening behavior? What about the common-law civil regulations that also accommodated and reinforced marriage? Should we resurrect actions for monetary damages for alienation of affection, breach of promise and seduction? Even if we did reinforce the law, given our culture, it would matter little in regard to how people behaved.

Divorce Reform Will Not Create Empathy

Given our current social climate, we are far beyond divorce reform as the means to address our family situations. Given that Americans are conditioned to think in terms of self-fulfillment, personal development and immediate gratification, we must question the continued viability of an institution idealistically defined by lifelong commitment and personal sacrifice.

Making divorce requirements more stringent will not magically transform the character of today's spouses. We are a self-centered people. There are no effective political appeals to empathy for others and no successful attempts to forge a sense of collective responsibility for the weaker members of society. Ours is a bleak and impoverished social vision in which "dependency" has become a dirty word used to stigmatize and an expression of "need" is understood as weakness. In reality, need and dependency are inevitable in the human condition.

High divorce rates are telling us that our society fails to value connectedness and commitment, the lack of which provides a good deal of the momentum behind the resort to divorce. For many Americans, sexual affiliations (of which marriage is but one—albeit the officially sanctified version) are the most tenuous of all intimate associations. If mates are not satisfactory, they can be discarded and new liaisons sought. To suppose that abolishing no-fault divorce will reverse the sexual revolution simply is wishful thinking. Our response to the high and relatively stable divorce rate should not be to advocate a return to some mythical past in which it is asserted that nuclear families thrived. Even if such a world once existed (and the evidence is overwhelmingly to the contrary), making divorce more difficult to obtain will not alter the fact that the aspirations and values of significant segments of the society have shifted. These new norms have undermined the continued viability of the traditional nuclear family model.

> *"Making divorce requirements more stringent will not magically transform the character of today's spouses."*

New Priorities

Making divorce harder to get will not undo the irrevocable evolution in women's expectations for themselves as members of families and as individuals within the larger society. In their historical roles as wives and mothers, women accepted with little questioning that they were the ones to bear the burdens of intimacy. However, continued self-sacrifice for husband and children in a society that increasingly makes it clear that it does not value noneconomic contributions and judges people by their material successes makes little sense. Women have had to change their behavior and set new priorities.

Young women in particular have internalized a norm of equality, with its attendant assumptions about career and political participation. They will not be relegated to a life that encompasses only hearth and home. They may want children, but they also want to be economically self-sufficient and not dependent on a husband for their well-being. With women's expectations for their "public" selves newly defined in the same terms as those for men, society no longer can safely assume that women will continue in the traditional role as an uncompensated family caretaker.

> *"To suppose that abolishing no-fault divorce will reverse the sexual revolution simply is wishful thinking."*

Thus, we find ourselves in the midst of historical behavioral changes affecting marriage and family. The implications of these changes are far-reaching but unclear. Conflict in established institutions and among individuals is inevitable. Internal contradictions are generated as women find themselves torn between the potent ideology associated with their traditionally defined family roles and the inherently just nature of their aspiration for equality. These conflicting and powerful messages often are impossible to reconcile, and choices must be made. Resolution may require the rejection of traditions and often results in rupturing existing relationships.

The End of the Traditional Family

Adding to the conflict is the fact that many men and most public and political institutions continue along as though no adjustments to the status quo are necessary. For example, women have received little support from political institutions when they have attempted to balance changing roles with a more equitable distribution of nurturing tasks. When women ask government for assistance with their traditional tasks of nurturing and caretaking, they find their requests for day care and family leave cast in political rhetoric as demands for special treatment or welfare handouts.

Empirical studies indicate that women have simply sacrificed leisure for market work while men's day-to-day lives have altered little. The workplace remains relatively unchanged, often presuming that workers have no outside demands. Removing no-fault divorce may sound like a quick legal fix, yet it does nothing to make marriage more attractive to today's women, who are commonly expected to continue as primary caregivers while they also are wage earners.

Within the traditional family, women's primary roles were those of wife and mother, supported by a breadwinner. But today, wives want to (or have to) work and are apt to be as career-minded as their husbands. Paradoxically, at the very moment in history that there has been such a profound change in expectations, women find they continue to provide the bulk of the caretaking tasks. They do so by default. Within many families, sustained help from male partners typically has been slow and often resentful in coming.

Men as well as women are leaving the traditional family—a cultural shift that divorce law cannot erase. Many men have reacted to women's changing aspirations and behavior by stubbornly holding on to the privileges they have enjoyed as the "head" of the family—a position around which other members organized their lives. Such men are unwilling to change. Some men leave old wives to look for more compliant (often younger) mates with whom they re-create the dream of a haven in a heartless world. Many women, responding to the profound contradiction between their newly forged expectations of equality and the reluctance of men and society to change, prefer to remain childless or become mothers without becoming (or remaining) wives.

The availability of no-fault divorce makes it easier to end marriages, but it does not explain the impetus behind the decisions to do so. Rather than trying to turn back the clock with revised divorce laws, we should move forward with a social commitment to support caretakers regardless of their marital status.

Many industrialized countries have child allowances to parents or mothers—whether married or not. By contrast, several states are pursuing welfare reforms that stigmatize unwed mothers and threaten to eliminate their payments by including "bridefare components." The government should give employers tax incentives to fund day care for all of their employees that parallel tax incentives for such items as research and product development. Congress should make as its first priority universal health care, including prenatal care. In addition, more liberal tax deductions should be allowed for people caring for elderly and disabled people, regardless of their family affiliation.

"We should move forward with a social commitment to support caretakers regardless of their marital status."

Behavior should be seen as adaptive—as a simple, evolutionary adjustment to the demise of the traditional nuclear family as an institution with well-defined gender roles for husbands and wives. Instead of casting the changing family and divorce as social "crises" and proposing punitive and unrealistic measures by crafting laws to compel people to conform to an outmoded model, law and policy should explicitly respond to the new social realities.

Divorce-Related Issues Should Be Settled Through Mediation

by Carl Wayne Hensley

About the author: *Carl Wayne Hensley is a professor of communications at Bethel College in St. Paul, Minnesota and adjunct professor at the University of St. Thomas.*

Editor's note: The following viewpoint was originally delivered as a speech before the graduate students in the Graduate School of Business at the University of St. Thomas in Minneapolis, Minnesota, on October 18, 1993.

When my wife filed for divorce, her attorney told her to go home and negotiate the division of the personal property with me. He told her that it would save her money. So, she was willing to negotiate with me on the house, the cars, the rental property, the antiques, and other tangible things. When we finished, both of us were satisfied with the division because we had full, equal input into that decision.

However, when she filed, she also asked for custody of our four-year-old daughter. I responded by asking for custody of our daughter. Now, neither her attorney nor mine nor anyone else told us that this *most crucial* issue might also be worked out like the property issues were worked out. So, our divorce went on the court calendar as a contested divorce. This meant that, before the divorce was settled, a social worker would conduct an investigation, and the judge would decide who would have custody of our daughter. At the last moment, I realized that I couldn't win. So, I told my attorney, "Tell her she can have custody; we won't go through an investigation." I certainly didn't like what happened. As a matter of fact, resentment and antagonism lurked in the shadows of our lives for a long time.

Now, my situation is not unique. If in the future a historian sits down at what will be the equivalent to a word processor in those days and writes a history of

From Carl Wayne Hensley, "Divorce—the Sensible Approach," speech delivered at the Graduate School of Business, University of St. Thomas, Minneapolis, Minnesota. Reprinted by permission.

the second half of the twentieth century, the 1980s and the 1990s could be labeled, "Decades of Divorce." We know that in the 80s divorce rates reached 50 percent, and that has continued during the 90s. We also know that about four-fifths of people who divorce the first time remarry, and almost 60 percent of those second marriages end in divorce. Divorce is so common that in an audience this size, some of you will have been touched by divorce. Maybe you are divorced yourself. Maybe your parents, maybe a brother

> *"Mediation provides a sensible approach to settling divorce-related issues."*

or sister, another relative, or a friend. It's just that common. Think about how continually antagonism, with his evil offspring resentment and conflict, stalks the land, taking his terrible toll on the lives of large numbers of people.

What divorcing people need is someone to help them steer their ship of life across the sea of matrimony so that when the hurricane of divorce sweeps over them, they'll not be swept onto the rocks and destroyed. I believe that mediation provides this kind of service. When I learned about mediation, I exclaimed, "Why didn't somebody tell me about this when I needed it?"

What is mediation? Mediation is a problem-solving approach in which the two parties engaged in a divorce work together to find mutual solutions to the problems and issues. They are guided by the mediator who is a neutral third party. With this guidance the couple takes responsibility for decisions which affect their lives; they create solutions; and they build ownership of the solutions. Therefore, I contend that *mediation provides a sensible approach to settling divorce-related issues.* That's really all I want to say to you tonight—mediation provides a sensible approach to settling divorce-related issues. I make this claim because of three distinct advantages which mediation offers to divorcing couples. Let's examine these advantages.

The Advantages of Mediation

First, mediation provides a sensible approach to settling divorce-related issues because it helps the couple manage their conflict. Separation and divorce create one of the most intense conflicts that human beings can experience. Love, warmth, and trust slowly evaporate, and disgust, detachment, anger, and suspicion rush in to take their place, like a tremendous, terrible cold front coming from the Arctic into Minnesota in the winter time. When managed in the typically competitive fashion, conflict is destructive. When managed in a *cooperative* fashion, it can be productive. So, mediation helps the couple to sort out the parts of the conflict so that they can manage it more positively.

When an individual enters a conflict, the common stance is to assume a position. "Here I stand, and I won't do anything else, and I won't accept anything else." But managing conflict from a position is difficult indeed because a position doesn't leave you much room to move and to make adjustments. Managing conflict from a position obscures the genuine interests that you have at stake.

It's much like driving on Minnesota freeways where tailgating seems to be a state hobby. Do you have that problem? You're driving along at 55 or 60 miles per hour; there's nobody else on the highway but you and the car behind you; and the car behind you is extremely close. I had such an experience a year or so ago. It was early winter. It was one of those misty, rainy, dark nights. I was driving on I-694, and a car pulled up behind me. I had my cruise control on somewhere between 55 and 60. The car pulled up behind me so close that I couldn't see his head lights in my rear view mirror, and I thought, "I don't like this." I eased off the accelerator so that he could pass me. However, he was so close to me that his car bumped my car at 55 miles an hour. If we'd had any kind of emergency, both of us could have been killed. Certainly, we would have had an accident because tailgating just doesn't leave any room to maneuver.

That's the way it is when you take a position—no room to maneuver. So, mediation helps the couple to explore the interests which lie beneath the positions. After all, interests are the energy sources that give positions their power over people. When you expose interests, you open up more options.

Working Through the Issues

I worked with a couple a few years ago, both in their late forties, married twenty-some years, three children around the age of twenty—a couple locked into rigid positions. They owned seven pieces of real estate: the homestead (the family home where she lived with the children), a house he bought after the separation in which he lived, and five pieces of rental property. She had been the stay-at-home mother, taking care of the children. He had a job with one of the big corporations in the city, had been with them for years, and had a substantial income. His position was that they should add up all their assets, subtract the debts, and divide net equity down the middle. In addition, (this was in November) he wanted to file a joint income tax return, and he wanted the $10,000 refund he thought he was going to get. That was it. He sat there and said, "That's the way it's going to be." She sat there and said, "I want these five pieces of property, and you can have the others." They'd had a temporary hearing, and he was paying temporary spousal maintenance. She said, "I will waive alimony." So there they sat. Hostility occasionally rose to the boiling point until one day, this physically big man exploded, stood up,

"As each spouse learns more [about the other's position], both become able to modify their defensive positions."

and threw his stack of documentation papers across my office. (I'm glad there was no history of physical abuse in that family because I really would have been scared.) He stood there for a few seconds and walked out.

Their positions were quite clear, but what do you suppose their interests were? Well, fortunately, I was able to help them uncover their interests. The wife was not concerned primarily with dollars. You see, when they separated, she had no marketable skills. She found a job doing menial clerk work, in the town in which they lived, at $10,000 a year. She knew that this was close to the limit of her earning ability and that the judge would probably give her permanent alimony. Do you know what she really wanted? Security. She wanted security which did not tie her to him. Alimony would have tied her to him for years to come. Moreover, she had managed the rental property through the years and knew that she could do it. That was her source of security—a security which in no way tied her to her husband.

> *"Most people do not want a knock-down-drag-out battle as part of a divorce."*

What did he want? I followed him out of my office and stood beside him on the driveway. As his anger slowly subsided, I said, "It really gets tough sometimes, doesn't it?" He said, "Yes, and you know what? I just want to come out of this with my dignity." His attorney was telling him what to do; his wife's attorney was telling him what to do; a judge had already told him in a temporary hearing what to do; his wife was telling him what to do. He simply wanted an agreement which reflected his input and which enabled him to salvage his self-esteem.

Once they were able to reframe their positions in terms of these issues, they worked out an acceptable agreement. They wouldn't have done that without mediation. The conflict would have continued to escalate and increase its destructive forces on both them and their children.

Managing Conflict

John Haynes, one of the earliest mediators in the country, said, "As each spouse learns more [about the other's position], both become able to modify their defensive positions," and thus increase their options. Divorce drives people into intense conflicts which can devastate unless managed properly. I really believe that most people do not want a knock-down-drag-out battle as part of a divorce. I have found that in all but a few cases couples still have remnant feelings of attachment and care. Mediation helps the couple manage conflict by helping them channel these remnant feelings toward resolving individual issues, thereby providing a sensible approach to settling divorce-related issues.

So, the first advantage of mediation is that it helps the couple manage conflict. The second advantage is that it helps the couple engage in a win-win exchange. Western culture in general, and American culture in particular, places a premium on winning. If you don't believe that, think about how athletics serve as metaphors for life in America. We don't like ties. In baseball we play extra innings. If it takes 25 innings, we play until there is a winner. In hockey—we play overtime. Football—we play overtime. Basketball—we play overtime.

Golf—we play extra holes. And, if we go through the overtimes and the extra holes, and there's still not a winner, we play "sudden death overtime." Think of the terminology and what it indicates. We place a premium on winning in spite of this great truth expressed by Harold Kushner: "To see the goal of life as winning forces us to see other people as competitors [and] threats to our happiness. . . . Their failure becomes [necessary for] our success." I said in my introduction that I relinquished my desire to have custody of my daughter because I knew I couldn't win. The legal system made me fully aware of this. Our legal system *nourishes* and *sustains* a win-lose approach to divorce.

Litigation escalates competition between two hurting, angry people. Our legal system is by nature adversarial. I heard Sandy Keith, the Chief Justice of the Minnesota Supreme Court, say, "A custody dispute is hell. Nothing is worse except war." And our legal system maintains and promotes this destructive competition. The competition increases until everything becomes an object to divide—houses, cars, children. The competition increases until it sometimes explodes in violence. [In 1992], Ramsey County Family Court judges began to initiate greater security measures including metal detectors, cameras, and electronic locks because of the increase in hostile behavior which divorce has brought to the courtroom. In Grand Forks, North Dakota, a man, summoned to court for failure to pay his child support payments, shot and critically wounded the judge. In a Fort Worth courtroom, a lawyer engaged in a bitter custody battle shot and killed two lawyers and wounded two judges.

> *"Mediators do not seek to replace lawyers. We seek to complement the work of lawyers."*

Although these are extreme cases, they are not uncommon. They are the result of a legal system which thrives on competition—a system which frequently destroys the few positive feelings which remain, causes blame casting, and leaves the individuals emotionally and, often, financially demolished.

A Win-Win Situation

Now, let me hasten to say that mediation does not seek to replace the lawyer. Lawyers are necessary because divorce is a legal matter. I advise couples who come to me, "If you don't have a lawyer, you need to get one. I'm not a lawyer, and you need to know your legal rights." Mediators do not seek to replace lawyers. We seek to complement the work of lawyers. The goal of mediation based on conflict management is not win-lose but agreement—an agreement which is shaped and shared by both spouses, and this creates a win-win situation.

Do you remember the childhood rhyme, "Jack Sprat could eat no fat, and his wife could eat no lean"? Well, in our competitive, win-lose legal system, one would have fared sumptuously and the other would have starved to death. But in a win-win system, "they licked the platter clean." So, mediation attempts to help the couple lick the platter clean by engaging in a win-win exchange. Mediation provides a sensible approach, then, to settling divorce-related issues because it helps manage conflict, and it helps the couple engage in a win-win exchange.

The third advantage of mediation is that it helps the couple stabilize personally as they deal with divorce decisions. An astute writer in the field of mediation is Isolina Ricci. She said simply, "Divorce is the most unfair process people experience." Mediation cannot anesthetize the pain of divorce. Mediation cannot make divorce more fair. Mediation cannot ease the agony of breaking up and starting over again. However, mediation can help to promote attitudes of respect for the other person as an individual of worth, honesty in the exchange, and concern for the future, and, thus, help the couple move toward stability.

Survival with Dignity

Sharon Lieblich, an attorney who specializes in domestic relations, pointed toward such stability when she said, "Try to look at it as a business deal. You want to minimize the amount spent on litigation, maximize the amount left, and finance the separation in the smartest way. The goal is survival with dignity." To stabilize personally means that the couple will have to reallocate resources and restructure the family significantly.

The stability that comes when they look at divorce as business and the decisions and issues of divorce as business decisions is absolutely essential when children are involved. Remember this, "Whom children join together, no divorce decree can put asunder." Mediation helps the couple to separate their roles as divorcing spouses from their roles as parents. Then, mediation seeks stability in their lives by helping them to rephrase the issues and view them differently. I firmly believe that language, to a great extent, shapes the perspectives or the viewpoints that we take.

So, take the language of divorce. Legally, we talk about "child custody." What does "custody" imply? Ownership, control, possession. We put criminals in custody. Thus, in mediation I tell couples, "When the divorce papers are drawn and when you go to court, they'll talk about 'custody.' Ignore that term. We're going to talk about 'parenting.' We're not going to talk about who the custodial parent is; we're going to talk about the places where the children live, and how much time the children live in Mom's house and how much time they live in Dad's house, and how that can be worked out to the advantage of the parents and the children." The legal system talks about parenting rights. In mediation I talk about parenting responsibilities and parenting privileges.

"Mediation can help to promote attitudes of respect for the other person as an individual of worth . . . and, thus, help the couple move toward stability."

Or take "visitation." Historically, the court has ordered that the mother have "custody" of the children and the father gets to "visit," usually two weekends a month and maybe one night a week. Well, visitation is something that outsiders do. Visitation is something strangers do. Visitation is something we do when we go to the funeral home to look at a dead body. So, in mediation, I don't talk about visitation. I never use that term. I talk about access. I talk about the children's access to both parents and the parents' access to the children.

> *"Mediation helps the couple to separate their roles as divorcing spouses from their roles as parents."*

Or take the term "child support"— historically, court ordered for the father. There are billions of dollars of court-ordered child support unpaid in this country, and thousands of children suffer because of it. There may be many reasons why it is unpaid, but one reason is because the man says, "No judge is going to tell me how to spend my money." In mediation I don't talk about child support. I tell them that it is a legal term used by lawyers and courts. Instead, I say, "Let's talk about the shared costs of rearing the children." I usually have them prepare a budget for the children. We go over that budget rigorously, and then *they* determine how much each partner is going to contribute to care for the children.

Beneficial Arrangements

The key questions are: (1) What arrangements will allow each spouse to be a loving, caring, nurturing parent? (2) What arrangements will enable these people to go through the devastating experience of divorce and survive as stable individuals? Mutually agreeable arrangements are absolutely essential—in property settlement, in spousal maintenance, and in child-parent relationships—if individuals are to reach a healthy level of stability.

Now, do you see why I assert that mediation provides a sensible approach for settling divorce-related issues? Do you see why I believe that mediation has to become a way of life in America when the divorce rate is so overwhelming? Do you understand that mediation helps the couple manage conflict, helps the couple engage in a win-win exchange, and helps the couple stabilize individually? Do you see more clearly that mediation does provide a sensible approach for settling divorce-related issues?

Joint Custody Should Be Encouraged

by Barbara Dority

About the author: *Barbara Dority is the president of Humanists of Washington, the executive director of the Washington Coalition Against Censorship, and cochair of the Northwest Feminist Anti-Censorship Taskforce.*

Many people who are concerned about social justice for women and children seem to be morally blind when it comes to the rights—if not the humanity—of divorced and separated fathers.

In today's social and political climate, it is not considered appropriate to speak in defense of divorcing and divorced men, or even of divorced fathers. This prevailing anti-male, anti-father attitude, employed in tandem with a lot of misinformation, flawed data, and sexist stereotypes, has succeeded in convincing most divorcing fathers that they are less than human. In the era of the "deadbeat dad," most believe that they cannot continue to be a father to their children after divorce and that they certainly couldn't perform adequately as a single parent. When contemplating the possibility of a separation or divorce, most involved fathers assume that they would forfeit their active parental role and become an every-other-weekend "visitor" in their children's lives. Beginning very early in the divorce process, fathers begin to receive consistent confirmation of this assumption.

Certainly some fathers voluntarily abdicate their parental responsibilities even in the absence of the many extenuating circumstances discussed below. Here, I address the tragic crisis faced by fathers who want very much to continue to parent their children after divorce.

Under current conditions, there are several reasons (other than the welfare of the children) for a wife to battle strenuously to obtain sole custody. The more custody the mother has of the child, the more financial support the courts will award her. Often, however, the main reason is totally unrecognized by the courts: the bitterness and need for revenge which attends so many marital

From Barbara Dority, "Civil Liberties Watch: Fathers Have Rights, Too," *Humanist*, March/April 1994. Reprinted by permission of the author.

breakups. Instead of recognizing the devastating effects this can have on everyone and attempting to minimize them, the legal system encourages the use of the children as weapons in divorce court.

Attorney Ronald K. Henry summed it up in testimony before a U.S. House subcommittee on June 30, 1992:

> We know that children are born with two parents. We know that children want, love, and need two parents. Still, we take two loving parents, we walk them into court at their most emotionally distraught and weak moment, and we say to them, "Here are your weapons. Fight it out and the last one standing owns the child."

The court system begins with the presumption that women are better suited to care for younger children than are men. Lawyers routinely tell divorcing fathers that they have very little chance of getting custody and that making the attempt will require thousands of dollars and a bitter court battle that will be very hard on all concerned, including the children.

Sexism in Custody Decisions

Just as many men have resisted giving up the economic advantages they have enjoyed, many women cling to their traditional domain of power. Various attempts are made to rationalize this behavior, such as the pervasive belief that men don't really want custody or continued involvement with their children. This is reminiscent of the arguments given for denying women full participation in economic life—and just as sexist.

When a marriage breaks up, regardless of the couple's financial and child-care arrangements, the courts presume that the wife has an equal right to the money and property her husband's and/or her labor has produced. Why isn't it also presumed that the father has equal rights to the children they have produced? If a father has participated in parenting—that is, child care and decisions regarding the children—why doesn't the father still have at least an equal right to continue parenting his children?

Instead, the system turns fathers into visitors with the every-other-weekend "privilege"—when mother sees fit to cooperate—to see his children. (In more than 20 states, visitation is legally defined as a "privilege" rather than a "right.") The mother makes all decisions about the children's education, health, religion, appearance, rules of behavior, and discipline. Only the mother is expected—or permitted—to participate in the daily development of the children.

> *"Why isn't it . . . presumed that the father has equal rights to the children [a couple has] produced?"*

Yet this system still demands his money. He becomes an economic object rather than a father. Like mothers, fathers accept the burdens of parenting so they can share in its rewards. But the system takes the rewards of parenthood from a divorcing father and leaves him with nothing *but* the burdens.

We know that there are three principal predictors of child-support compliance: the fairness of the original court order, access to the children, and employment stability. Regardless, the divorced father is expected to maintain his children's standard of living *and* support a separate life for himself. Sometimes this is genuinely impossible, because support payments are set with no provisions for economic realities such as unemployment, underemployment, or serious accident or illness. And second families are not taken into account.

Child-support enforcement is the most punitive form of debt collection in America. A billion-dollar collection bureaucracy has been created that exists for no other form of private debt collection. Tax refunds are intercepted, liens are imposed, credit is ruined, professional licenses and drivers' licenses are revoked, and people are thrown in jail. (Debtors' prisons live.) These gross violations of civil liberties, which would not be tolerated in any other situation, are also self-defeating methods of collection. Nevertheless, "enforcement" continues.

We hear much about the Bureau of Census statistics, which allegedly reveal that only 50 percent of support is paid in full and that 25 percent is paid only in part. Despite the fact that these numbers have been questioned by several independent researchers over the years, they are still accepted as accurate. One researcher and analyst, Professor Sanford Braver, has exposed incredible methodological errors in the gathering of this data.

> *"The system takes the rewards of parenthood from a divorcing father and leaves him with nothing but the burdens."*

There is no verification of amounts (women were asked simply how much they receive; noncustodial parents were not asked for corroboration, nor were court records checked); nothing is done to correct obvious sources of false data (for example, the known tendency of welfare recipients to underreport outside income); no data is gathered on how many nonpaying or underpaying noncustodial parents are unemployed, underemployed, disabled, supporting second families, or withholding payment because they are not permitted to see their children.

Incredibly, no distinction is made between child support ordered after divorce and support for children whose fathers are *unknown* to their mothers. In other words, in many cases these "deadbeat dads" don't even *know* they are fathers, and many more are under 18 years of age. These statistics even fail to exclude obligors who are dead!

Professor Braver points out:

> Buried in the data is a very interesting fact which received no publicity from special interest groups or from the federal enforcement program. Sixty-six percent of noncompliance was reported by the custodial mothers themselves as "father unable to pay."

And even with all its methodological flaws, the Census Bureau data show that access to the children makes the biggest difference. Over 90 percent of support was paid in joint-custody situations where both parents were permitted to continue to be parents.

Both Parents Must Be Involved

If we are really concerned about the welfare of children, we must start working on a system that encourages the continued involvement of both parents after divorce. We must abandon distorted stereotypes and the band-aid policies which treat only the symptoms of the problem.

A friend whose work I much admire, Professor Ferrel Christensen, founder of the Canadian Movement to Establish Real Gender Equality, writes with simple eloquence:

> Justice is not an intellectual exercise. It is still being denied all around us, causing vast amounts of human misery. Sexism in parenting must be brought to an end.

Joint Custody Should Not Be Encouraged

by David Sheff

About the author: *David Sheff is a freelance writer.*

My son began commuting between his two homes at age 4. He traveled with a Hello Kitty suitcase with a pretend lock and key until it embarrassed him, which was long before it wore out. He graduated to a canvas backpack filled with a revolving arsenal of essential stuff: books and journals, plastic vampire teeth, "Star Trek" Micro Machines, a Walkman, CDs, a teddy bear.

The commuter flights between San Francisco and Los Angeles were the only times a parent wasn't lording over him, so he was able to order Coca-Cola, verboten at home; flight attendants didn't care about cavities. But such benefits were insignificant when contrasted with his preflight nightmares about plane crashes.

One winter he was to fly not to Los Angeles but to New York, where his mother and stepfather were spending Christmas. During the preparations for the visit, he learned that he would have to change planes en route. Late at night, long after I had put him to bed, he crept into the living room and climbed onto my lap, trembling. When I asked him what the matter was, he said, "I don't want to change planes."

I told him not to worry, but he was unconvinced. Amid sobs, he asked, "What if I fall off the wing?"

"What will you be doing on the wing?"

"Changing planes," he said. "I might fall off when I'm walking from one to the other."

Like so many divorcing couples, we divided the china and art and our young son. Joint custody was the obvious approach; Nicolas's mother and I both wanted him and had no reason to doubt the prevailing wisdom that it would be best for him to continue to be raised by both parents. An evaluator helped us determine the details of his schedule, and the shuttle began. First he was ferried back and forth between our homes across town, and then, when his mother moved to Los Angeles, across the state. For the eight years since, he has been one of the thousands of American children with two homes, two beds, two sets of clothes and toys and two toothbrushes.

Each year more than a million children see their parents divorce. Most of them will be raised primarily by one parent, usually the mother. But by one estimate, divorce decrees provide for the parental joint custody of approximately 100,000 to 200,000 children annually. A study of 1,124 families who had filed for divorce in two Northern California counties, conducted between 1984 and 1988 by Eleanor Maccoby, a psychologist at Stanford and Robert Mnookin, a professor of law at Harvard, determined that 16.8 percent of the families who had completed divorce proceedings had children living in joint physical custody.

> *"Joint custody is sometimes imposed on the very children most likely to be hurt by it."*

Here and throughout this viewpoint, I am referring to joint physical custody arrangements in which children live for substantial amounts of time with each parent. The arrangement takes innumerable forms: some children, for example, spend the school week with one parent and the weekends with the other. Other children may switch as often as every three or four days. Distance can make some arrangements seem particularly torturous. One young boy was ordered by the court to live part of each month with his father in San Mateo, Calif., and the remainder with his mother, 400 miles south in San Diego, simultaneously enrolled in two schools. There are children who spend six months with each parent and others who alternate yearly. One of my son's friends has a schedule so complex it is tracked by a secretary, who types out a new calendar each month.

The Rise of Joint Custody

Up until the mid-19th century, children in the rare divorce remained with their father. According to Mary Ann Mason, professor of law and social welfare at Berkeley and author of *From Father's Property to Children's Rights*, "children were viewed as his assets, valuable as workers, whether in the fields or factories." With the decline of child labor, they ended up at home, in their mother's care, and this helped form the basis of the modern bias. Though fathers occasionally retain custody, it is still the exception.

The concept of sole custody—which usually meant mother custody—went virtually unchallenged until the 1970's. The women's movement denounced it because full-time moms—single or remarried, who often received little or no child support—had their hands full, with little time to pursue careers or other interests. Fathers, meanwhile, actively rebelled against the prejudice that often cut them off from their children. Consequently, many therapists, mediators, judges, and parents came to view joint custody as the best resolution in most cases. Particularly embraced by men's groups, it became the modern, enlightened choice. Yet today there is little convincing evidence that joint custody is the best arrangement for the children, in fact there is mounting evidence to show that it can, in some cases, be the worst.

Comparative studies, though scarce, indicate that these children fare no better than children in the sole custody of their father or mother. In certain circumstances, they do much worse. In fact, joint custody is sometimes imposed on the very children most likely to be hurt by it. The divorces that end up in litigation are usually the hostile ones, and judges sometimes impose joint custody because it favors neither parent. Janet Johnston of the Center for the Family in Transition in Marin County, Calif., studied 100 children whose embattled parents were litigating custody in court. The children, ages 12 and under, were evaluated over four years, beginning in 1982. Johnston and her colleagues determined that how a child fares after divorce depends on several critical factors: the intensity of the parents' battles during the marriage and since the divorce, the degree to which the children became involved in the parents' disputes, the amount of shared time they had with both parents and the number of times the child was shuttled between homes. When children in joint custody had more frequent access to both parents and were systematically exposed to their parents' battles, they were in worse shape than the kids in sole custody, suffering from overly aggressive behavior, sleeping problems, withdrawal, depression and eating difficulties. The findings, the study concluded, "indicate that recommending or ordering joint custody or frequent visitation in these cases is contraindicated"—basically, a bad idea.

An Altered Concept of Home

Beyond placing children in what one therapist describes as "no man's land," joint custody fundamentally alters the concept of home. Indeed, "homes" is an antilogy. How many adults can imagine having two primary homes? For children, home is even more important, the psychological and physical cradle of development, the brick-and-mortar incarnation of all that their parents represent: stability, safety and the rules of life. Joint custody presupposes that children can do just as well when they are divided between two homes, each home defined by a different parent, and perhaps stepparents and stepsiblings, as well as a jumble of often contradictory expectations and values.

> *"Joint custody fundamentally alters the concept of home."*

Certainly joint custody provides children with a semblance of stability—if it's Tuesday it must be Dad's house. But there is also a built-in instability, with weekly (or whatever) departures, arrivals and transitions; and then, just when the children settle in, it's time to leave again. Some children are apparently flexible enough to adapt, but others become traumatized. Their parents are able to move on with their lives after a divorce, but the children's efforts to do so are continually undermined.

Judith Wallerstein, founder of the Center for the Family in Transition, has observed young boys and girls who, upon returning from one to the other parent's home, wander from object to object—table to bed to sofa—touching them seemingly to affirm that they are still there. The absent parent may seem even more elusive than the furniture. Although children no longer require tactile proof as they grow older, they may incorporate a sense that both of their homes are illusory and impermanent. Some children, Wallerstein says, "perceive that there is a mom's home and a dad's home, but not a child's home. You'd like to think that these kids could simply integrate their lives between their two homes, have two sets of peers, and easily adjust to being with each parent. But most children do not have the flexibility. They begin to feel as if it's a flaw in their character, when it is simply impossible for many people to conduct parallel lives."

> *"Children [living in joint custody] may incorporate a sense that both of their homes are illusory and impermanent."*

Nicolas has lived in joint custody for the past eight years, and you would think he would be used to it by now. He is not. His emotional preparation begins a week or so before he flies to visit his mother. (Nicolas lives with me when he is in school.) He becomes, to varying degrees, anxious, lethargic, somber and withdrawn from his friends. The back and forth seems only to have become tougher on him as he has grown older.

In response, his mother and I recently modified the schedule so that Nick will be separated from his friends for shorter periods of time. He is happy about the change. Nevertheless, he is not sanguine about the arrangement; it remains the most difficult aspect of his life, more difficult than the divorce was. Though he would never want to have to choose between his parents, neither would he choose joint custody.

And neither would I choose it for him if I had the chance to make the decision again. Yes, it has contributed to his character. He is probably more responsible, sensitive, worldly, introspective and sagacious than he might have otherwise been. But the toll has been such that, given the geographic and emotional chasms of our divorce, his mother and I should have agreed on sole custody. If we had not been able to agree, it should have been imposed. Though it would have been devastating for the one of us who lost custody of our son, I am convinced that Nicolas's childhood would have been easier. Instead, he is left with a meager consolation prize for all his commuting between parents. He has more frequent-flier miles than most adults.

Sole-Custody Decisions Should Be Gender-Neutral

by Dorsett Bennett

About the author: *Dorsett Bennett is an attorney in Roswell, New Mexico.*

Divorce is a fact of modern life. A great number of people simply decide that they do not wish to stay married to their spouse. A divorce is not a tremendously difficult situation unless there are minor children born to the couple. If there are no minor children you simply divide the assets and debts. But you cannot divide a child. The child needs to be placed with the appropriate parent.

In my own case, my former wife chose not to remain married to me. That is her right and I do not fault her decision. My problem is that I do not believe it is her right to deny me the privilege of raising our children. Some fathers want to go to the parent/teacher conferences, school plays, carnivals and to help their kids with homework. I have always looked forward to participating on a daily basis in my children's lives. I can no longer enjoy that privilege—the children live with their mother, who has moved to a northern Midwest state.

I tried so hard to gain custody of my children. I believe the evidence is uncontradicted as to what an excellent father (and more important, parent) I am. My ex-wife is a fairly good mother, but unbiased opinions unanimously agreed I was the better parent. Testimonials were videotaped from witnesses who could not attend the out-of-state custody hearing. I choose to be a father. When I was 3 years old, my own father left my family. While I've loved my father for many years, I did and still do reject his parental pattern.

A couple of centuries ago, a father and mother might have shared equally in the care and raising of children above the age of infancy. But with the coming of the Industrial Revolution the father went to work during the day, leaving the full-time care of the young to the mother, who stayed at home. It was easier to decide who should get child custody under those circumstances. That would be true today even if the mother were put into the position of working outside the home after the divorce.

Now, a majority of married mothers are in the workplace—often because the family needs the second income to survive. With the advent of the working mother, we have also seen a change in child care. Not only have we seen an increase in third-party caregivers; there is a decided difference in how fathers interact with their children. Fathers are even starting to help raise their children. I admit that in a great many families there is an uneven distribution of child-care responsibilities. But there are fathers who do as much to raise the children as the mother, and there are many examples where men are full-time parents.

The Favored Parent

But, because we have this past history of the mother being the principal child caregiver, the mother has almost always been favored in any contested child-custody case. The law of every state is replete with decisions showing that the mother is the favored custodial parent. The changes in our lifestyles are now being reflected in our laws. In most, if not all, states, the legislature has recognized the change in child-care responsibilities and enacted legislation that is gender blind. The statutes that deal with child custody now say that the children should be placed with the parent whose care and control of the child will be in the child's best interest.

This legislation is enlightened and correct. Society has changed. We no longer bring up our children as we did years ago. But it is still necessary to have someone make the choice in

> *"There are fathers who do as much to raise the children as the mother."*

the child's best interest if the parents are divorcing and cannot agree on who takes care of the kids. So we have judges to make that enormous decision.

The state legislature can pass laws that say neither parent is favored because of their gender. But it is judges who make the ultimate choice. And those judges are usually *older males* who practiced law during the time when mothers were the favored guardians under the law. These same judges mostly come from a background where mothers stayed home and were the primary caregivers. By training and by personal experience they have a strong natural bias in favor of the mother in a child-custody case. That belief is regressive and fails to acknowledge the changed realities of our present way of life. Someone must be appointed to render a decision when parents cannot agree. I would ask that those judges who make these critical decisions re-examine their attitudes and prejudices against placing children with fathers.

The Better Parent Should Receive Custody

After the videotaped testimony was completed, one of my lawyers said he had "never seen a father put together a better custody case." "But," he asked me, "can you prove she is unfit?" A father should not be placed in the position of having to prove the mother is unfit in order to gain custody. He should not have to prove that she has two heads, participates in child sacrifice or eats live snakes. The father should only have to prove that he is the more suitable parent.

Fathers should not be discriminated against as I was. It took me three years to get a trial on the merits in the Minnesota court. And Minnesota has a law directing its courts to give a high priority to child-custody cases. What was even worse was that the judge seemed to ignore the overwhelming weight of the evidence and granted custody to my ex-wife. At the trial, her argument was, "I am their mother." Other than that statement she hardly put on a case. Being the mother of the children was apparently deemed enough to outweigh evidence that all the witnesses who knew us both felt I was the better parent; that those witnesses who knew only me said what an excellent parent I was; that our children's behavior always improved dramatically after spending time with me; that my daughter wished to live with me, and that I had a better child-custody evaluation than my wife.

> *"A father should not be placed in the position of having to prove the mother is unfit in order to gain custody."*

So I say to the trial judges who decide these cases: "Become part of the solution to this dilemma of child custody. Don't remain part of the problem." It is too late for me. If this backward way of thinking is changed, then perhaps it won't be too late for other fathers who should have custody of their children.

Chapter 4

Should Gay Marriage Be Legalized?

CURRENT CONTROVERSIES

Same-Sex Marriage: An Overview

by Richard Stengel

About the author: *Richard Stengel is a senior writer for* Time.

IT IS BETTER TO MARRY THAN TO BURN.—*Paul*, I Corinthians 7:9

The funny thing is, on the issue of same-sex marriage, both sides agree with Paul. In fact, advocates of same-sex marriage and their opponents concur that it is better to marry than almost anything else. They both embrace the idea that marriage is the bedrock of a stable society, and that it is the ideal method of civilizing wayward and wanton males, something every society must do. In short, hooray for till-death-us-do-part. The only problem is that both sides disagree vehemently on who should be allowed to take that vow.

Compared with, say, the federal deficit or welfare, the issue of same-sex marriage is not exactly a crisis in the Republic. But it has become a hot campaign issue because of a 1993 Hawaiian supreme court ruling that denying marriage licenses to gay couples may violate the equal-protection clause in the state constitution. Sending the case back to the trial court, the supreme court directed the government to show that it has a "compelling" state interest in maintaining the ban—a test it is unlikely to meet. Although the case is . . . on appeal in a state court in Honolulu, Hawaii will probably rule . . . that such marriages are permissible. Christian conservatives, in particular, are worried that if gay marriages are allowed in Hawaii, the Full Faith and Credit clause in Article IV of the U.S. Constitution would require every other state to recognize the legitimacy of such unions. . . .

The Hawaiian case has stirred fury in statehouses across the country. Thirty-five states have considered legislation against same-sex marriage, with 11 states enacting such bans and 17 refusing to do so. . . . President Clinton announced that if Congress passed the Defense of Marriage Act to deny federal recognition to same-sex marriages, cosponsored by Bob Dole, Clinton would say "I do" and sign it. Presumably the move would show that he is not beholden to the homosexual community. The President chose to make the point just after the U.S. Supreme Court . . . struck down a Colorado law nullifying civil-rights protection for homosexuals, a decision viewed as a significant victory for gay rights.

Whatever the electoral points to be gained on it, same-sex marriage is less a political issue than a moral, philosophical and legal one. The debate on precisely those grounds has engaged prominent thinkers on both sides.

NEVER MARRY BUT FOR LOVE.—*William Penn*

One of the most persuasive advocates of same-sex marriage is Andrew Sullivan, the departing editor of the *New Republic*. His writings suggest the following syllogism: Marriage is for people who love; homosexuals love; ergo marriage is for them. He and others push the argument further by claiming that denying homosexuals access to this fundamental societal institution is a denial of their civil and human rights. Citing the philosopher Hannah Arendt, who proposed same-sex marriage in a pioneering 1959 essay, Sullivan suggests that the right to marry whomever one wishes is an elementary human right, part of the Declaration's inalienable right to life, liberty and the pursuit of happiness—or a long-term partner, as the case may be.

> *"[Andrew Sullivan's] writings suggest the following syllogism: Marriage is for people who love; homosexuals love; ergo marriage is for homosexuals."*

Advocates also argue that legalizing gay unions is a way of getting the spousal benefits—health insurance, pension plans, inheritance rights—that long-term domestic partners deserve. Moreover, Sullivan maintains that marriage will encourage care giving to partners, something especially vital in the age of AIDS.

One of the fundamental contentions of Sullivan and other same-sex advocates is that marriage—for homosexuals as well as heterosexuals—"domesticates" young men. Even the eminent social scientist James Q. Wilson asserts that nothing beats marriage for civilizing men, something every culture must find a way to do. Sullivan asserts marriage is such an important investment in social stability that the benefits to society outweigh any real or imagined harm.

IF A MAN ALSO LIE WITH MANKIND, AS HE LIETH WITH A WOMAN, BOTH OF THEM HAVE COMMITTED AN ABOMINATION.— Leviticus 20:13

The primary argument against same-sex marriage is really a religious animus against homosexuality. In short, homosexuality is a grave sin in the eyes of God and should not be condoned or comforted by the mystical union of marriage, which is a covenant with God. Opponents of same-sex marriage point to the fact that disapproval of homosexual behavior is one of the most deeply rooted and consistent moral teachings in Jewish, Christian and Muslim traditions.

THE FIRST BOND OF SOCIETY IS MARRIAGE.—*Cicero*, De Officiis

Cicero's statement reflects what is known as the natural-law argument against same-sex unions. This is the idea that marriage evolved in society over thousands of years as a childbearing union between a man and a woman, and that there is a profound wisdom in the tradition that should not be lightly discarded. Virtuecrat William J. Bennett contends that same-sex marriages "would do significant long-term social damage" to "society's most important institution." And that stretching the definition of marriage would jeopardize an already shaky institution.

The Christian right takes this belief a step further, suggesting that gay activists are in fact attempting to poison the youth of America with same-sex propaganda. Christian conservatives fear that children are being exposed to gay alternatives too early in life, when they are not old enough to make a mature judgment about their own inclinations. The Utah legislature recently passed a bill banning gay clubs in state high schools. And at Merrimack High School in New Hampshire, teachers have stopped using a film on the life of Walt Whitman because it mentions he was gay.

THE NATURAL AND INHERENT RIGHT OF MARRIAGE . . . WHICH IS TO INCREASE AND MULTIPLY.—*Pope Leo XIII*

Sullivan answers those who argue that marriage is for procreation by saying that same-sex marriage is no different from sterile or elderly heterosexuals' marrying. Why should they have the right to marry and not homosexuals? But social scientist Wilson believes the raising of children remains the central role of marriage because "we have found nothing else that works as well." Besides, both Bennett and Wilson say, Sullivan undermines his own argument that the absence of children should not be an impediment to gay marriages when he says that it will give gay couples "greater freedom" to enjoy "extramarital outlets." Marriage, Bennett says, is not an open construct; "its essential idea is fidelity."

> *"The primary argument against same-sex marriage is [that] . . . homosexuality is a grave sin in the eyes of God."*

MARRIAGE—WHAT AN ABOMINATION! LOVE—YES, BUT NOT MARRIAGE.—*George Moore*

Some gay activists spurn the idea of same-sex marriage, suggesting that homosexuals are buying into the corrupt ideology of an outworn institution. Writing in the New York *Times*, author Frank Browning maintained, "The problem is with the shape of marriage itself. What we might be better off seeking is civic and legal support for different kinds of families that can address the emotional, physical and financial obligation of contemporary life." This is the idea that endorsing marriage is endorsing the traditions of a society that explicitly rejects homosexuality. In other words, don't join them if you can't beat them.

Chapter 4

THE WEDLOCK OF MINDS WILL BE GREATER THAN THAT OF
BODIES.—*Erasmus*

   Despite the glaring differences between the two sides, there is a corner of
consensus. Both sides are united in the desire to strengthen the foundations of
civil society. But is there a way to accomplish this in a manner that satisfies all
concerned? Is there an evolutionary middle ground? Is it not possible, for example, to be against discrimination toward homosexuals yet not in favor of gay
marriage? Compromises are already taking shape. Some cities, including New
York, offer bereavement leave and health insurance to the domestic partners of
city employees. Stuart Kelman, a Conservative rabbi in Berkeley, California,
has proposed an alternative to traditional religious marriage: a ceremony for
what he calls a "covenant of love" for couples wishing to sanctify lifelong
monogamous relationships. Ancient Roman law recognized three categories of
marriage—a legally sanctioned union, marriage by purchase and marriage by
mutual consent. Perhaps states might recognize different types of unions for
both same-sex and heterosexual partnerships.
   One conviction shared by both sides is that love, not law, conquers all. Sullivan writes that the heart of both marriage and being human is "the ability to
love and be loved." State representative Ed Fallon of Iowa, who opposed a bill
outlawing same-sex marriage, noted afterward, "There isn't a limited amount of
love in Iowa. It isn't a nonrenewable resource." It is one natural resource that
neither side need be shy about exploiting.

Government Should Not Recognize Same-Sex Marriage

by Bob Barr

About the author: *Bob Barr is a U.S. representative from Georgia and a sponsor of the Defense of Marriage Act.*

The enduring significance of the institution of marriage was posed in three lines from Samuel Butler's epic, *Hudibras*, well over three centuries ago: "For in / What stupid age or nation / Was marriage ever out of fashion?"

Well, we now know the answer to Butler's query: Hawaii, 1996.

I was stunned to learn that Hawaii is close to giving legal recognition to homosexual marriages. It all began in 1991 when three homosexual couples sued the state of Hawaii, arguing that Hawaii's exclusion of same-sex couples from the statutory definition of marriage was invalid either under the U.S. Constitution or the Hawaii Constitution. When the lawsuit goes to trial in the summer of 1996, a Hawaii trial court is expected to rule in favor of the couples. [The court legalized same-sex marriages in December 1996, ruling that banning the marriages was unjustified discrimination.]

The Definition of Marriage

This led me to think that I might have slept through one or more of my law classes at Georgetown University 20 years ago. So, I pulled out my 1968 edition of *Black's Law Dictionary* to look up the legal definition of "marriage." My memory did not fail me. The law dictionary defined marriage as "the civil status, condition or relation of one man and one woman united in law whose association is founded on the distinction of sex." Wanting to be certain the intervening 20 years had not wrought an upheaval in this legal institution, I checked a current law dictionary, several other dictionaries, a thesaurus and an encyclopedia. All backed up my recollection of marriage as a legally recognized and

From Bob Barr, "No: Don't Let Homosexual Activity Subvert the Cornerstone of Civilized Society," *Insight*, June 10, 1996. Reprinted by permission of *Insight* magazine; ©1996 News World Communications, Inc. All rights reserved.

judicially preferred union of a man and a woman.

In remembering this definition of the term I am not alone. Marriage always has commonly and legally been recognized as the union of a man and a woman, not a man and a man or a woman and a woman. The regulation—and protection—of that marriage relationship has been a fundamental obligation of government since before Christ. Aristotle recognized this more than 2,000 years ago, and our Supreme Court has done so consistently throughout our own history. The high court has ruled consistently that marriage is a fundamental liberty that cannot be denied, for example, on account of race.

> *"Marriage always has commonly and legally been recognized as the union of a man and a woman."*

If one reviews the long line of Supreme Court cases recognizing the importance to our society of marriage as its cornerstone, one rarely will find the justices taking the time to note, in their opinions, that the term "marriage" means a union between a man and a woman. They don't do so because there has been no need to do so; it has been self-evident through all of modern history. No longer.

In just one generation, homosexual activists have, through political power and intimidation—and cleverly crafted court challenges—created the need for the Supreme Court to confront the obvious and reaffirm it. Thus, the court in 1986 faced the question of whether the Constitution granted a fundamental and protected right to engage in homosexual behavior. In that case, involving a challenge to Georgia's sodomy laws, the court found that not only was there no such constitutionally guaranteed right to homosexual behavior, but also that such behavior could not be used as the basis for marriage.

One might think that would have been the end of the matter. Not so. The battle goes on and we must confront the challenge. If we don't, or if we fail, the door will have been blasted open to challenges to laws outlawing polygamy and sexual relations between adults and children and to laws limiting marriage to people not closely related. If the homosexuals successfully defeat the legal recognition of marriages as limited to heterosexual couples and replace it with the "any loving relationship" pabulum they spout, marriage will become meaningless. And, once that happens, it will be virtually impossible to place any other limits on marriage or sexual relations.

Of course, the advocates of same-sex marriage retort: Why place limits? Why stop "normal" behavior? You see, in their view, those who believe in maintaining the institution of heterosexual marriage in the America of 1996 are the "extremists," because they see themselves as "normal." I have been labeled an extremist by letters I have received since introducing the Defense of Marriage Act. This is rather odd, given the fact that the president has indicated through White House spokesman Michael McCurry that he supports the measure. Bill Clinton, an extremist?

The fact of the matter is that homosexual behavior is not normal behavior. Homosexual activists are asking us to "normalize" abnormal behavior, even though, by definition, it just can't be done. And we are being asked to believe that same-sex marriages will bring every group in society closer together. Ah yes, and we will all go off in the sunset with birds singing, with no more wars and no more hatred, because homosexual couples can now marry each other.

Perhaps some same-sex advocates are naive enough to believe this utopian nonsense, but, when all is said and done, homosexual advocates are simply seeking more power—political, economic and cultural. Unfortunately, through inaction or conflict avoidance, government at every level already has surrendered a great deal of power to the vanguard of the homosexual revolution. But now homosexual culture warriors are at the castle gates. There are no more lines in the sand to be erased.

Is there an appropriate role for the Congress; one that does not meddle in the affairs of the states; one that respects principles of federalism? Yes, there is. *Congress is, should and must be* a part of this battle. We have no choice in view of the fact that homosexual activists intend to take marriage licenses granted homosexual couples in Hawaii as early as the summer of 1996, travel elsewhere and challenge other states to recognize their same-sex marriages under the full-faith-and-credit clause in Article 4, Section 1 of the Constitution. Thus, once Hawaii recognizes same-sex marriages, other states will be asked to do the same, with unpredictable results.

Although the homosexual activists plan to use the full-faith-and-credit clause as a legal sledgehammer, the very same provision of the Constitution provides the rest of us the weapon to defeat them. The final clause explicitly grants the Congress the power to determine the "effects" of the provision.

The Defense of Marriage Act

The Defense of Marriage Act, which [Bill Clinton signed into law in September 1996], addresses this threat to the basic building block of society in the most appropriate, direct and limited way possible. It is a reaction to extremists, not an overreaction.

> *"If the homosexuals successfully defeat the legal recognition of marriages as limited to heterosexual couples . . . , marriage will become meaningless."*

The Defense of Marriage Act does not force any view of marriage on any state. It does not force any state to define marriage in one way or another. It presumes—perhaps erroneously, insofar as recent polls suggest that by a wide margin even the citizens of Hawaii do not agree that legal status ought to be granted same-sex marriages—that each state will continue to define marriage in heterosexual terms as its citizens wish.

The proposed law addresses two limited but important issues. First, it says that no state can be forced, under the full-faith-and-credit clause, to accept the notion of same-sex marriage. The act would recognize that if citizens of my home state of Georgia, for example, don't want to accept same-sex marriages, we don't have to; no matter what the courts in Hawaii decide. In this sense, the Defense of Marriage Act is, pure and simple, a defense of state's rights.

> *"Homosexual behavior is not normal behavior."*

It is essential that Congress take this action. We simply cannot rely upon the federal courts to protect state policies from an overextension of the full-faith-and-credit clause. And, like some Hawaii state judges, some of today's federal judges also are capable of bizarre rulings. Witness the refusal of a federal judge in New York to admit into evidence 80 pounds of cocaine found in the trunk of a defendant's car.

One Man and One Woman

Second, in exercising its legitimate role of defining the scope of federal laws and privileges, the Defense of Marriage Act defines "marriage" as the union of one man and one woman only, for purposes of federal—not state—laws. This is important, for example, to prevent homosexual couples from abusing federal-benefits laws intended for husbands and wives.

Some in Congress as well as their ultraliberal allies will try to convince a majority in the Congress and the president that "marriage" means anything and, therefore, nothing. I don't believe they will succeed. On the other hand, if someone had suggested to me 10 years ago that some of our courts would sanction same-sex marriages and that the national media would demonize those who argued against such "marriages," I would have said they were crazy. Yet, here we are, facing just such a cultural onslaught by extremists. Lawmakers cannot stand on the sidelines and assume that marriage, the building block of society, will endure this latest siege intact.

Marriage Is Not a Fundamental Right

by Mona Charen

About the author: *Mona Charen is a nationally syndicated columnist.*

The Hawaii Supreme Court could, if it rules in favor of same-sex marriages, plunge the United States into a constitutional pickle. [A Hawaiian trial court ruled in December 1996 that Hawaii could not prohibit gay couples from receiving marriage licenses.]

The full faith and credit clause of the Constitution reads as follows: "Full Faith and Credit shall be given in each State to the public Acts, Records, and judicial Proceedings of every other State." At first glance, that would seem to seal the case. If gay marriages become valid in Hawaii, then gay couples from around the nation could fly there, be married and return home as husband and husband, or wife and wife, and the other 49 states would be obliged to recognize those marriages as valid.

Not a Basic Right

But the Constitution goes on to say, "And the Congress may by general Laws prescribe the Manner in which such Acts, Records and Proceedings shall be proved, and the Effect thereof."

A good many constitutional scholars think the second sentence opens the door to national legislation that could limit the legitimacy of same-sex marriages to Hawaii. The Defense of Marriage Act, which would do just that, is currently wending its way through Congress. [Bill Clinton signed the Defense of Marriage Act in September 1996.]

The arguments on behalf of same-sex marriage have been cast—as so many debates in America are—as a matter of "rights" and "discrimination." The Equal Marriage Rights Home Page on the World Wide Web, for example, proposes the following resolution: "Because marriage is a basic human right and an individual personal choice, RESOLVED, the State should not interfere with same-gender couples who choose to marry and share fully and equally in the

From Mona Charen, "Marriage Isn't a Basic Human Right," *Conservative Chronicle*, July 17, 1996. Reprinted by permission of Mona Charen and Creators Syndicate.

rights, responsibilities and commitment of civil marriage."

Where to begin? Marriage is not a basic human right. Though it conduces to the happiness of men and women, it is not primarily designed for them. It is designed for children. To say that the state ought not to "interfere" with same-sex couples who choose to marry is meaningless. Marriage is something the state confers because it wants to reward certain kinds of behavior. Marriage between men and women, tested over centuries, has been judged to promote a healthy society. Within families created by traditional marriage, children are raised to be good citizens of the larger society.

The state does not currently "interfere" in homosexual relationships (nor should it). But to demand the "right" to marry is to ask more than that the state refrain from interference; it is to ask the state to confer a benefit.

Mothers and Fathers

But what good will the state be achieving for itself if it confers the benefit of marriage on homosexuals? Homosexual unions do not advance the interests of the larger society. They do not result in the birth of children.

What about adoption? If the state permits homosexuals to marry, it can hardly discriminate against them when it comes to adoption. Would it be desirable to have significant numbers of children raised by homosexual couples?

The pop answer is that love solves everything. As long as a child gets love, what does it matter whether it comes from two mommies or two daddies?

> *"Marriage is something the state confers because it wants to reward certain kinds of behavior."*

It matters a lot. We are learning from the epidemic of divorce and illegitimacy just how important it is to grow up with one parent of each sex. Girls without fathers are far more likely than those who grow up with both parents to get pregnant, bear illegitimate children, have trouble in school and have difficulty forming lasting relationships. Boys who grow up with a mother alone are more likely to have trouble in school, break the law, experiment with drugs and commit suicide than those who grow up with both parents.

In a million ways, some subtle, some obvious, men and women contribute different things as parents. Mothers tend to be more protective and nurturing; fathers more playful and challenging. Mothers say, "Be careful on that jungle gym." Fathers say, "How high can you go?" Fathers give daughters a sense of attractiveness and self-confidence. Mothers show their sons how to treat a lady. Mothers teach girls how to become women. Fathers show boys what it means to be a man.

Homosexual Relationships Are Not Marriages

Relationships between those of the same sex cannot be marriages. A marriage is the foundation of a family. They are instead friendships. Let's leave it at that.

The Purpose of Marriage Is Procreation

by *Commonweal*

About the author: Commonweal *is a biweekly Catholic magazine.*

There is every likelihood that Hawaii's Supreme Court will soon overturn that state's prohibition on same-sex marriage. [A Hawaiian trial court legalized same-sex marriages in December 1996.] The court's reasoning will be simple enough: Hawaii's constitution forbids discrimination on the basis of sex, and for the state to deny the benefits of marriage to same-sex couples without demonstrating a "compelling state interest" does precisely that. Should Hawaii license same-sex marriage, other states may be bound to recognize those marriages under the Full Faith and Credit clause of the Constitution. The U.S. Supreme Court, it seems certain, will eventually be asked to rule on the constitutionality of the heterosexual exclusivity of marriage.

For the state to license same-sex unions will entail a fundamental reappraisal of the nature of marriage and the balance struck between rights of individual self-determination and the integrity of basic social institutions such as the family. American society has much to gain from a fair-minded debate about such questions, and much to lose if we retreat further from reasoning together about the nature and aims of our common life.

The Nature of Marriage

Whether there are compelling enough reasons to preserve the heterosexual exclusivity of marriage is a question that arises in the wake of profound changes in how we think about sexual morality, procreation, and marriage. Historically, marriage forged a powerful connection between sexual love, procreation, and the care of children. However, contemporary understandings of marriage increasingly stress the primacy of individual self-fulfillment, not intergenerational attachments. Moreover, contraception and abortion have essentially severed any unwilled connection between sex and procreation. That connection has been further attenuated by technological advances allowing us to separate biological, gestational, and relational parenting at will. In this context, marriage's meaning seems anything but secure.

But is a further erosion of marriage's traditional linkage between sexual love and human procreation desirable? Advocates of same-sex marriage advance two arguments. First, denying same-sex couples the marriage rights enjoyed by heterosexual persons is discriminatory, an imposition of unjustified inequality. Second, same-sex marriage is presented as an embrace of, not an assault on, what is acknowledged to be a uniquely valuable social institution. If society wishes to promote the human goods of marriage—emotional fulfillment, lifelong commitment, the creation of families, and the care of children—marginalizing homosexuals by denying civil standing to their publicly committed relationships makes little sense, advocates argue.

> *"Same-sex marriage, like polygamy, would change the very nature and social architecture of marriage."*

In modern democratic societies wide latitude is given to individuals and groups pursuing often conflicting and incompatible conceptions of the good. Still, a broad tolerance and a high regard for individual autonomy cannot result in the equal embrace of every private interest or social arrangement. Economic freedom, for example, must be balanced against environmental concerns. Parents' rights to instill their own values in their children must accommodate the state's mandate to set educational standards for all children. The exclusive legal status of monogamous marriage, it is useful to remember, was once challenged by Mormon polygamy. But polygamy was judged inimical to the values of individual dignity and social comity that marriage uniquely promotes.

Marriage Would Change

Now we must weigh the implicit individual and social benefits of heterosexual marriage against those of same-sex unions. In this light, advocates of same-sex marriage often argue that laws prohibiting it are analogous to miscegenation statutes. But the miscegenation analogy fails. Miscegenation laws were about racial separation, not about the nature of marriage. Legalizing same-sex unions will not remedy a self-evident injustice by broadening access to the traditional goods of marriage. Rather, same-sex marriage, like polygamy, would change the very nature and social architecture of marriage in ways that may empty it of any distinctive meaning.

Recent social history can guide us here. Proponents of no-fault divorce argued that the higher meaning of marriage, and even the health of children, would be better served in making marriage easier to dissolve. Yet the plight of today's divorced women and their children refutes such claims. In fact, the loosening of marital bonds and expectations has contributed to the devaluation and even the abandonment of the marriage ideal by many, while encouraging unrealistic expectations of marriage for many more. How society defines marriage has a profound effect on how individuals think and act. And how individuals fashion their most intimate relationships has an enormous impact on the quality of our common life. The dynamic involved is subtle, but real.

Should marriage be essentially a contractual arrangement between two individuals to be defined as they see fit? Or does marriage recognize and embody larger shared meanings that cannot be lightly divorced from history, society, and nature—shared meanings and social forms that create the conditions in which individuals can achieve their own fulfillment? Popular acceptance of premarital sex and cohabitation gives us some sense of the moral and social trajectory involved. Both developments were welcomed as expressions of greater honesty and even better preparations for marriage. Yet considerable evidence now suggests that these newfound "freedoms" have contributed to the instability and trivialization of marriage itself, and have not borne the promises once made for them of happier lives. Similarly, elevating same-sex unions to the same moral and legal status as marriage will further throw into doubt marriage's fundamental purposes and put at risk a social practice and moral ideal vital to all.

The Procreative Marriage

The heterosexual exclusivity of marriage can be defended in the same way social policy rightly shows a preference for the formation of intact two-parent families. In both cases, a normative definition of family life is indispensable to any coherent and effective public action. Certainly, mutual love and care are to be encouraged wherever possible. But the justification and rationale for marriage as a social institution cannot rest on the goods of companionship alone. Resisting such a reductionist understanding is not merely in the interests of heterosexuals. There are profound social goods at stake in holding together the biological, relational, and procreative dimensions of human love.

"There are countless ways to 'have' a child," writes theologian Gilbert Meilaender of the social consequences and human meaning of procreation (*Body, Soul, & Bioethics*, University of Notre Dame Press, 1996). "Not all of them amount to doing the same thing. Not all of them will teach us to discern the equal humanity of the

> *"Marriage as a social form is first a procreative bond."*

child as one who is not our product but, rather, the natural development of shared love, like to us in dignity. . . . To conceive, bear, give birth to, and rear a child ought to be an affirmation and a recognition: affirmation of the good of life that we ourselves were given; recognition that this life bears its own creative power to which we should be faithful."

Is there really any doubt that in tying sexual attraction to love and love to children and the creation of families, marriage fundamentally shapes our ideas of human dignity and the nature of society? Same-sex marriage, whatever its virtues, would narrow that frame and foreshorten our perspective. Marriage, at its best, tutors us as no other experience can in the given nature of human life and the acceptance of responsibilities we have not willed or chosen. Indeed, it should tutor us in respect for the given nature of homosexuality and the dignity of homosexual persons. With this respect comes a recognition of difference—a difference with real consequences.

> *"We are all the offspring of a man and a woman, and marriage is the necessary moral and social response to that natural human condition."*

Still, it is frequently objected that if the state does not deny sterile or older heterosexual couples the right to marry, how can it deny that right to homosexual couples, many of whom are already rearing children?

Exceptions Prove the Rule

Exceptions do not invalidate a norm or the necessity of norms. How some individuals make use of marriage, either volitionally or as the result of some incapacity, does not determine the purpose of that institution. In that context, heterosexual sterility does not contradict the meaning of marriage in the way same-sex unions would. If marriage as a social form is first a procreative bond in the sense that Meilaender outlines, then marriage necessarily presupposes sexual differentiation, for human procreation itself presupposes sexual differentiation. We are all the offspring of a man and a woman, and marriage is the necessary moral and social response to that natural human condition. Consequently, sexual differentiation, even in the absence of the capacity to procreate, conforms to marriage's larger design in a way same-sex unions cannot. For this reason sexual differentiation is marriage's defining boundary, for it is the precondition of marriage's true ends.

Same-Sex Marriage Will Degrade Marriage

by Charles Krauthammer

About the author: *Charles Krauthammer is a well-known writer whose essays have appeared in* Time, Newsweek, *and the* New Republic.

The House of Representatives may have passed legislation . . . opposing gay marriage, but the people will soon be trumped by the courts. In September the judges of the Hawaii Supreme Court are expected to legalize gay marriage. Once done there, gay marriage—like quickie Nevada divorces—will have to be recognized "under the full faith and credit clause of the Constitution" throughout the rest of the U.S.

Gay marriage is coming. Should it?

For the time being, marriage is defined as the union 1) of two people 2) of the opposite sex. Gay-marriage advocates claim that restriction No. 2 is discriminatory, a product of mere habit or tradition or, worse, prejudice. But what about restriction No. 1? If it is blind tradition or rank prejudice to insist that those who marry be of the opposite sex, is it not blind tradition or rank prejudice to insist that those who marry be just two?

In other words, if marriage is redefined to include two men in love, on what possible principled grounds can it be denied to three men in love?

This is traditionally called the polygamy challenge, but polygamy—one man marrying more than one woman—is the wrong way to pose the question. Polygamy, with its rank inequality and female subservience, is too easy a target. It invites exploitation of and degrading competition among wives, with often baleful social and familial consequences. (For those in doubt on this question, see *Genesis: 26-35* on Joseph and his multimothered brothers.)

The question is better posed by imagining three people of the same sex in love with one another and wanting their love to be legally recognized and socially sanctioned by marriage.

Why not? Andrew Sullivan, author of *Virtually Normal: An Argument About*

Homosexuality, offers this riposte to what he calls the polygamy diversion (*New Republic*, June 7): homosexuality is a "state," while polygamy is merely "an activity." Homosexuality is "morally and psychologically" superior to polygamy. Thus it deserves the state sanction of marriage, whereas polygamy does not.

But this distinction between state and activity makes no sense for same-sex love (even if you accept it for opposite-sex love). If John and Jim love each other, why is this an expression of some kind of existential state, while if John and Jim and Jack all love each other, this is a mere activity?

And why is the impulse to join with two people "morally and psychologically inferior" to the impulse to join with one? Because, insists Sullivan, homosexuality "occupies a deeper level of human consciousness than a polygamous impulse." Interesting: this is exactly the kind of moral hierarchy among sexual practices that homosexual advocates decry as arbitrary and prejudiced.

Finding, based on little more than "almost everyone seems to accept," the moral and psychological inferiority of polygamy, Sullivan would deny the validity of polygamist marriage. Well, it happens that most Americans, finding homosexuality morally and psychologically inferior to heterosexuality, would correspondingly deny the validity of homosexual marriage. Yet when they do, the gay-marriage advocates charge bigotry and discrimination.

Or consider another restriction built into the traditional definition of marriage: that the married couple be unrelated to each other. The Kings and Queens of Europe defied this taboo, merrily marrying their cousins, with

> *"If marriage is redefined to include two men in love, on what possible principled grounds can it be denied to three men in love?"*

tragic genetic consequences for their offspring. For gay marriage there are no such genetic consequences. The child of a gay couple would either be adopted or the biological product of only one parent. Therefore the fundamental basis for the incest taboo disappears in gay marriage.

Do gay-marriage advocates propose to permit the marriage of, say, two brothers, or of a mother and her (adult) daughter? If not, by what reason of logic or morality?

The problem here is not the slippery slope. It is not that if society allows gay marriage, society will then allow polygamy or incest. It won't. The people won't allow polygamy or incest. Even the gay-marriage advocates won't allow it.

The point is *why* they won't allow it. They won't allow it because they think polygamy and incest wrong or unnatural or perhaps harmful. At bottom, because they find these practices psychologically or morally abhorrent, certainly undeserving of society's blessing.

Well, that is how most Americans feel about homosexual marriage, which constitutes the ultimate societal declaration of the moral equality of homosexuality and heterosexuality. They don't feel that way, and they don't want society to say so. They don't want their schools, for example, to teach their daughters that society is entirely indifferent whether they marry a woman or a man. Given the choice between what Sullivan calls the virtually normal (homosexuality) and the normal, they choose for themselves, and hope for their children, the normal.

They do so because of various considerations: tradition, utility, religion, moral preference. Not good enough reasons, say the gay activists. No? Then show me yours for opposing polygamy and incest.

Homosexual Love Is Not True Love

by Donald DeMarco

About the author: *Donald DeMarco is an author and lecturer.*

Love, which characterizes the essence of God and, as Dante states, moves the sun and the stars, is probably the world's most dangerous euphemism. What is labelled as love can very easily turn out to be something far less noble: lust, self-indulgence, infatuation, or even a political strategy. Some of the strangest things that take place are done in the name of love.

What Is Love?

How do we know, then, that what we call "love" really is love? This is one of the fundamental questions that has challenged the minds of the great philosophers. Aristotle argued that love must promote the good of the beloved. Augustine taught that it must be consistent with the love of God. Aquinas spoke of it terminating in a union with the loved one.

Taking the thoughts of these three philosophers collectively, we can depict love as an act which promotes the good of another in a way that not only is harmonious with our love for God, but also with the love we have for ourselves and our loved ones with whom we seek to be united. Love is not love, therefore, unless it properly orders and balances ourselves, our loved ones, nature, and God. Love is not merely an impulse, it is an intensely realistic and balanced set of relationships that promotes the good of all concerned.

The image of marriage described in Genesis 1:28, in which man and woman become two-in-one-flesh and are commanded to be fruitful and multiply, accords on the highest level with this notion of love.

Homosexual groups, currently extremely powerful both politically and in the media, have been advancing the notion that sexual acts between members of the same sex can be just as loving as those between husband and wife. Love is universal in that it transpires between any human beings. Mothers love their daughters, fathers their sons, siblings each other, and neighbors love their

From Donald DeMarco, "Testing Love's Impulse," *Family*, June 1993. Reprinted with permission of the author.

neighbors independently of sex, race, creed, class, or nationality. But as soon as the dimension of sex enters the picture, the question of order arises: is the order that sex sets in motion consistent with the good of all who are involved? Incest, fornication, adultery, bigamy, polyandry, sadomasochism, and so on, involve sex in ways that are clearly disharmonious with the goods of all who are involved.

> *"Homosexual activity cannot lead to the conception of new life."*

One man may love another man, or a woman may love another woman, but the sexual component does not offer them a means whereby they can confer real goods upon each other. The Vatican's Pastoral Letter on homosexuality (*The Pastoral Care of Homosexuals*, 1987) fully recognizes that homosexual persons are often generous and giving of themselves. But at the same time, it states that "when they engage in homosexual activities they confirm within themselves a disordered sexual inclination which is essentially self-indulgent."

Homosexual activity cannot lead to the conception of new life. In this regard, it lacks one level of ordination that would clearly carry it beyond the level of self-indulgence. By the same token, however, the use of contraception, sterilization, and abortion among heterosexuals can render their sex acts equally self-indulgent. The need for a proper moral order applies to heterosexuals as much as it does to homosexuals.

The Physical Benefits of Heterosexual Sex

In another line of ordination, heterosexual intercourse confers mutual physiological and endocrinological benefits upon the partners that homosexual congress cannot. As a result of natural intercourse, husband and wife exchange hormones and other factors, which once assimilated into the body, confer upon each other important benefits. Accordingly, F.X. Arnold has written: "The transmission of the hormonal exchange appears to be part of the vital basis for the satisfying functioning of other physical and emotional processes which are necessary for a harmonious married life" (*Woman and Man: Their Nature and Mission*, Herder, 1963, p. 3).

A key to understanding the natural benefits that husband and wife give each other as a result of intercourse is the normal functioning of the immune system. Male semen contains a mild immunosuppressant which suppresses the woman's immune or defense system just enough to allow the two partners to achieve a two-in-one-flesh union. From a strict immunological standpoint, male sperm and consequent embryos are seen as foreign bodies. The purpose of the immune system is to protect the body against anything that is foreign to it. But the immunosuppressant contained in semen changes that and allows for a true and complete union to be achieved between the husband and the wife and then the embryo and the mother. Thus, the immunosuppressant instructs the woman's immune system to treat both her husband's sperm and her future un-born child not as agents against which she must be defended but as agents with which she is to be united.

Homosexual congress disrupts the normal functioning of the immune system. Among the adverse effects is the possibility of contracting AIDS, which renders the immune system dysfunctional. Because AIDS was first established among sexually promiscuous homosexuals, it was initially termed GRID, standing for Gay Immunodeficiency Disease. It was changed to AIDS as a result of lobbying done by homosexual medical activists.

AIDS is without question a great harm. The notion that homosexual activity is harmless is naivete in the extreme. Knowledge of the immune system and how it responds differently with regard to hetero- and homosexual activity elu-cidates the life and death differences inherent in these two radically divergent modes of sexual behavior. In this vein, a San Francisco journalist has pondered: "Isn't it something that what brought most of us here now leaves tens of thou-sands of us wondering whether that celebration ends in death."

When we think of harm, we usually first think of it in a physical sense where it is immediate, apparent, and specific. Moral harm (and the physi-cal harm it later brings) is initially delayed, non-apparent, and non-specific (consider the delayed but devastating guilt of Lady Macbeth). This is not surprising since moral

> *"Homosexual coupling can hardly be characterized as love since it does not enter into that web of ordination that gives marriage its life, depth, and even divinity."*

harm involves our whole being and has a spiritual component which is not al-ways readily identifiable. Many people may think that homosexual acts do not harm anyone simply because the harm is not immediately experienced.

Homosexuals and Love

Marriage demands permanence, fidelity, generosity, openness to life, and no end of additional moral virtues. Homosexual coupling can hardly be character-ized as love since it does not enter into that web of ordination that gives mar-riage its life, depth, and even divinity.

G.K. Chesterton once said that the man who is knocking on the door of a brothel is looking for God. All of our impulses, in the final analysis, are ordi-nated to God. What makes life so problematic is the disorders that move in the opposite direction where there is no ultimate satisfaction or point of rest.

We all have an impulse to love, but unless it is properly ordered—that is, di-rected toward God who is the author of Life and Love—it will betray us. A truer test of love than an appeal to mere feeling (or political expediency) is whether it is ordered to the goods of self, other, neighbor, community, and God.

Homosexuals Should Be Allowed to Marry

by *The Economist*

About the author: *The* Economist *is a conservative British weekly news-magazine.*

Marriage may be for the ages—but it changes by the year. And never, perhaps, has it changed as quickly as since the 1960s. In western law, wives are now equal rather than subordinate partners; interracial marriage is now widely accepted both in statute and in society; marital failure itself, rather than the fault of one partner, may be grounds for a split. With change, alas, has come strain. In the 25 years from 1960, divorce rates soared throughout the west—more than sextupled in Britain, where divorce appears inevitable for the world's most celebrated marriage, that of Charles and Diana Windsor. [Their divorce was granted in the summer of 1996.] Struggling to keep law apace with reality, Britain's Tory government is even now advancing another marriage reform, seeking, on the whole sensibly, to make quick or impulsive divorce harder but no-fault divorce easier.

That, however, is not the kind of reform which some decidedly un-Tory people are seeking—and have begun to achieve. Denmark, Norway and Sweden now allow homosexual partners to register with the state and to claim many (though not all) of the prerogatives of marriage. The Dutch are moving in the same direction. In France and Belgium, cities and local governments have begun recognising gay partnerships. And, in the American state of Hawaii, a court case may legalise homosexual marriage itself. [A Hawaiian court legalized homosexual marriage in December 1996.]

As of today, however, there is no country which gives homosexuals the full right of marriage. And that is what gay activists in more and more places are seeking. Marriage, one might think, is in turbulent enough waters already. Can gay marriage be a good idea—now?

To understand why the answer is yes, first set aside a view whose appealing simplicity is its undoing. "Governments are not elected to arrange nuptial liaisons, much less to untangle them," writes Joe Rogaly in the [London] *Financial Times*. "It is a purely private matter." On this libertarian view, the terms of a marriage contract should be the partners' business, not the state's. With the help of lawyers and sympathetic churchmen, homosexuals can create for themselves what is in all practical respects a marriage; if they lack a government licence, so what?

The government-limiting impulse motivating this view is admirable. But, in truth, the state's involvement in marriage is both inevitable and indispensable. Although many kinds of human pairings are possible, state-sanctioned marriage is, tautologically, the only one which binds couples together in the eyes of the law. By doing so it confers upon partners unique rights to make life-or-death medical decisions, rights to inheritance, rights to share pensions and medical benefits; just as important, it confers upon each the legal responsibilities of guardianship and care of the other. Far from being frills, these benefits and duties go to the very core of the marriage contract; no

> *"Homosexuals need emotional and economic stability no less than heterosexuals— and society surely benefits when they have it."*

church or employer or "commitment ceremony" can bestow them at one blow. If marriage is to do all the things that society demands of it, then the state must set some rules.

Just so, say traditionalists: and those rules should exclude homosexuals. Gay marriage, goes the argument, is both frivolous and dangerous: frivolous because it blesses unions in which society has no particular interest; dangerous because anything which trivialises marriage undermines this most basic of institutions. Traditionalists are right about the importance of marriage. But they are wrong to see gay marriage as trivial or frivolous.

Society's Stake in Marriage

It is true that the single most important reason society cares about marriage is for the sake of children. But society's stake in stable, long-term partnerships hardly ends there. Marriage remains an economic bulwark. Single people (especially women) are economically vulnerable, and much more likely to fall into the arms of the welfare state. Furthermore, they call sooner upon public support when they need care—and, indeed, are likelier to fall ill (married people, the numbers show, are not only happier but considerably healthier). Not least important, marriage is a great social stabiliser of men.

Homosexuals need emotional and economic stability no less than heterosexuals—and society surely benefits when they have it. "Then let them 'unchoose' homosexuality and marry someone of the opposite sex," was the old answer. Today that reply is untenable. Homosexuals do not choose their condition; indeed, they often try desperately hard, sometimes to the point of suicide, to avoid it. However, they are less and less willing either to hide or to lead lives of celibacy. For society, the real choice is between homosexual marriage and homosexual alienation. No social interest is served by choosing the latter.

To this principle of social policy, add a principle of government. Barring a compelling reason, governments should not discriminate between classes of citizens. As recently as 1967, blacks and whites in some American states could not wed. No one but a crude racist would defend such a rule now. Even granting that the case of homosexuals is more complex than the case of miscegenation, the state should presume against discriminating—especially when handing out something as important as a marriage licence. Thus the question becomes: is there a compelling reason to bar homosexuals from marriage?

One objection is simply that both would-be spouses are of the same sex. That is no answer; it merely repeats the question. Perhaps, then, once homosexuals can marry, marital anarchy will follow? That might be true if homosexual unions were arbitrary configurations, mere parodies of "real" marriage. But the truth is that countless homosexual couples, especially lesbian ones, have shown that they are as capable of fidelity, responsibility and devotion as are heterosexual couples—and this despite having to keep their unions secret, at least until recently. Would gay marriage weaken the standard variety? There is little reason to think so. Indeed, the opposite seems at least as likely: permitting gay marriage could reaffirm society's hope that people of all kinds settle down into stable unions.

The question of children in homosexual households—adoption, especially— is thorny. That question, however, is mainly separate from the matter of marriage as such. In settling a child with guardians who are not the natural parents, the courts and adoption agencies will consider a variety of factors, just as they do now; a couple's homosexuality may be one such factor (though it need not, by itself, be decisive).

In the end, leaving aside (as secular governments should) objections that may be held by particular religions, the case against homosexual marriage is this: people are unaccustomed to it. It is strange and radical. That is a sound argument for not pushing change along precipitously. Certainly it is an argument for legalising homosexual marriage through consensual politics (as in Denmark), rather than by court order (as may happen in America). But the direction of change is clear. If marriage is to fulfill its aspirations, it must be defined by the commitment of one to another for richer for poorer, in sickness and in health— not by the people it excludes.

Same-Sex Marriage Is Fair

by E.J. Graff

About the author: *E.J. Graff is writing a book,* What Is Marriage For?

The right wing gets it: Same-sex marriage is a breathtakingly subversive idea. So it's weirdly dissonant when gay neocons and feminist lesbians publicly insist—the former with enthusiasm, the latter with distaste—that same-sex marriage would be a conservative move, confining sexual free radicals inside some legal cellblock. It's almost as odd (although more understandable) when pro-marriage liberals ply the rhetoric of fairness and love, as if no one will notice that for thousands of years marriage has meant Boy+Girl=Babies. But same-sex marriage seems fair only if you accept a philosophy of marriage that, although it's gained ground in the past several centuries, still strikes many as radical: the idea that marriage (and therefore sex) is justified not by reproduction but by love.

Changing the Message

Sound like old news? Not if you're the Christian Coalition, the Pope or the Orthodox rabbinate, or if you simply live in one of many pre-industrial countries. Same-sex marriage will be a direct hit against the religious right's goal of re-enshrining biology as destiny. Marriage is an institution that towers on our social horizon, defining how we think about one another, formalizing contact with our families, neighborhoods, employers, insurers, hospitals, governments. Allowing two people of the same sex to marry shifts that institution's message.

That's why the family-values crowd has trained its guns on us, from a new hate video called *The Ultimate Target of the Gay Agenda: Same Sex Marriages* to the apocalyptically named Defense of Marriage Act. [The Defense of Marriage Act, signed into law by Bill Clinton in September 1996, gives federal recognition of marriage only to those composed of one man and one woman.] The right wing would much rather see outré urban queers throwing drunken kisses off bar floats than have two nice married girls move in next door, with or without papoose, demonstrating to every neighborhood kid that a good marriage is defined from the inside out, that sodomy is a sin only in the mind of the beholder.

From E.J. Graff, "Retying the Knot," *Nation*, June 24, 1996. Reprinted with permission from the *Nation* magazine; © The Nation Company L.P.

Chilled by that coming shift, antimarriage conservatives have also been disingenuous in their arguments, which basically come down to crying "tradition!" like a Tevye chorus. Even a quick glance at social history shows what conservatives pretend isn't so: Very little about marriage is historically consistent enough to be "traditional." That it involves two people? Then forget the patriarch Jacob, whose two wives and two concubines produced the heads of the twelve tribes. That it involves a religious blessing? Not early Christian marriages, before marriage was a sacrament. That it is recognized by law? Forget centuries of European prole "marriages" conducted outside the law, in which no property was involved. That it's about love, not money? So much for centuries of negotiation about medieval estates, bride-price, morning gift and dowry (not to mention bride-burnings in today's India). Those who tsk away such variety, insisting that everyone knows what marriage *really* is, miss the point. Marriage is—marriage always has been—variations on a theme. Each era's marriage institutionalizes the sexual bond in a way that makes sense for that society, that economy, that class.

So what makes sense in ours? Or, to put it another way, what is contemporary marriage for? That's the question underlying the debate as right-wing and gay activists prepare for Hawaii's aftermath. [A Hawaiian trial court legalized same-sex marriage in December 1996.] Its answer has to fit our economic lives. In a G.N.P. based on how well each of us plumbs our talents and desires in deciding what to make, buy or sell, we can hardly instruct those same innards to shut up about our sexual lives—as people could in a pre-industrial society where job, home and religion were all dictated by history. The right wants it both ways: Adam Smith's economy *and* feudal sexual codes. If same-sex marriage becomes legal, that venerable institution will ever after stand for sexual choice, for cutting the link between sex and diapers.

Ah, but it already does. Formally, U.S. marriage hasn't been justified solely by reproduction since 1965, when the Supreme Court batted down the last laws forbidding birth control's sale to married couples. In Margaret Sanger's era, contraception was charged with "perversion of natural functions," "immorality"

> *"Each era's marriage institutionalizes the sexual bond in a way that makes sense for that society, that economy, that class."*

and "fostering egotism and enervating self-indulgence." Dire diseases were predicted for those who indulged. Those are, almost word for word, the charges hurled by every critic of homosexuality—and for the same reasons. Once their ideologies are economically outdated, what can conservatives invoke except the threat of divine judgment?

All of which is why same-sex marriage is being considered in every post-industrial country, and why it seems simply "fair" to so many, including Hawaii's Supreme Court. That sense of fairness also draws on the liberal idea that a pluralist democracy's institutions should be capacious, that civic marriage should be one-size-fits-all. But same-sex marriage does more than just fit; it announces that marriage has changed shape.

The Benefits

As with any social change, there will be more consequences, which look pretty progressive to me. There are practical benefits: the ability to share insurance and pension benefits, care for our ill partners, inherit automatically, protect our children from desperate custody battles. And marriage will end a negative: Our sexual lives can no longer be considered felonious, which stings us in fights ranging from child custody to civil rights. A more notable progressive shift is that, since same-sex couples will enter the existing institution, not some back-of-the-bus version called "domestic partnership" or "queer marriage," marriage law will have to become gender-blind. Once we can marry, jurists will have to decide every marriage, divorce and custody question (theoretically at least) for equal partners, neither having more historical authority. Our entrance might thus rock marriage more toward its egalitarian shore.

> *"If same-sex marriage becomes legal, that venerable institution will ever after stand for sexual choice, for cutting the link between sex and diapers."*

Some progressives, feminists and queer nationalists nevertheless complain that instead of demanding access to the institution as it is, we should be dismantling marriage entirely. But lasting social change evolves within and alters society's existing institutions. No one will force same-sex couples to darken the institution's doors; we'll merely gain the choices available to heterosexual pairs. None of this will alter a hard fact of contemporary life: Every commitment—to job, spouse, community, religion—must be invented from the inside out. Making lesbians and gay men more visible legally will insist that there is no traditional escape: that our society survives not by rote but by heart.

Gay Marriage Will Not Degrade Marriage

by Andrew Sullivan

About the author: *Andrew Sullivan is the author of* Virtually Normal: An Argument About Homosexuality *and the former editor of the* New Republic.

It wasn't that we hadn't prepped. Testifying on the Hill was a first for me, and those of us opposing the "Defense of Marriage Act" had been chatting for days about possible questions. But we hadn't quite expected this one. If a person had an "insatiable desire" to marry more than one wife, Congressman Bob Inglis of South Carolina wanted to know, what argument did gay activists have to deny him a legal, polygamous marriage? It wasn't a stray question. Republican after Republican returned gleefully to a Democratic witness who, it turned out, was (kind of) in favor of polygamy. I hastily amended my testimony to deal with the question. Before long, we were busy debating on what terms Utah should have been allowed into the Union and whether bisexuals could have legal harems.

Riveting stuff, compared to the Subcommittee on the Constitution's usual fare. But also revealing. In succeeding days, polygamy dominated the same-sex marriage debate. Both Bill Bennett and George Will used the polygamy argument as a first line of defense against same-sex marriage. In the *Washington Post* and *Newsweek*, Bennett in particular accused the same-sex marriage brigade of engaging in a "sexual relativism" with no obvious stopping place and no "principled ground" to oppose the recognition of multiple spouses.

False Assumptions

Well, here's an attempt at a principled ground. The polygamy argument rests, I think, on a couple of assumptions. The first is that polygamous impulses are morally and psychologically equivalent to homosexual impulses, since both are diversions from the healthy heterosexual norm, and that the government has a role to prevent such activities. But I wonder whether Bennett really agrees with this. Almost everyone seems to accept, even if they find homosexuality morally troublesome, that it occupies a deeper level of human consciousness than a

From Andrew Sullivan, "Three's a Crowd," *New Republic*, June 17, 1996. Reprinted by permission of the *New Republic*, ©1996, The New Republic, Inc.

polygamous impulse. Even the Catholic Church, which believes that homosexuality is an "objective disorder," concedes that it is a profound element of human identity. It speaks of "homosexual persons," for example, in a way it would never speak of "polygamous persons." And almost all of us tacitly assume this, even in the very use of the term "homosexuals." We accept also that multiple partners can be desired by gays and straights alike: that polygamy is an *activity*, whereas both homosexuality and heterosexuality are *states*.

> *"Polygamy is an* activity, *whereas both homosexuality and heterosexuality are* states.*"*

So where is the logical connection between accepting same-sex marriage and sanctioning polygamy? Rationally, it's a completely separate question whether the government should extend the definition of marriage (same-sex or different-sex) to include more than one spouse or whether, in the existing institution between two unrelated adults, the government should continue to discriminate between its citizens. Politically speaking, the connection is even more tenuous. To the best of my knowledge, there is no polygamists' rights organization poised to exploit same-sex marriage to return the republic to polygamous abandon. Indeed, few in the same-sex marriage camp have anything but disdain for such an idea. And, as a matter of social policy, same-sex marriage is, of course, the opposite of Bennett's relativism. Far from opening up the possibilities of multiple partners for homosexuals, it actually closes them down.

Bennett might argue, I suppose, that any change in marriage opens up the possibility of any *conceivable* change in marriage. But this is not an argument, it's a panic. If we're worried about polygamy, why not the threat of legally sanctioned necrophilia? Or bestiality? The same panic occurred when interracial marriage became constitutional—a mere thirty years ago—and when women no longer had to be the legal property of their husbands. The truth is, marriage has changed many, many times over the centuries. Each change should be judged on its own terms, not as part of some seamless process of alleged disintegration.

Monogamy and Adultery

So Bennett must move to his next point, which is that homosexuals understand the institution of marriage so differently than heterosexuals do that to admit them into it would be to alter the institution entirely. To argue this, he has to say that gay men are so naturally promiscuous that they are constitutively unable to sustain the monogamous requirements of marriage and so fail to meet the requirements of membership. He has even repeatedly—and misleadingly—quoted my book, *Virtually Normal*, to buttress this point.

Bennett claims that I believe male-male marriage would and should be adulterous—and cites a couple of sentences from the epilogue to that effect. In context, however, it's clear that the sentences he cites refer to some cultural differences between gay and straight relationships, as they exist today *before same-sex marriage has been made legal*. He ignores the two central chapters of my book—and several articles—in which I unequivocally argue for monogamy as central to all marriage, same-sex or opposite-sex.

That some contemporary gay male relationships are "open" doesn't undermine my point; it supports it. What I do concede, however, is that, in all probability, gay male marriage is not likely to be identical to lesbian marriage, which isn't likely to be identical to heterosexual marriage. The differences between the genders, the gap between gay and straight culture, the unique life experiences that divide as well as unite heterosexuals and homosexuals, will probably create an institution not easily squeezed into a completely uniform model. And a small minority of male-male marriages may perhaps fail to uphold monogamy as successfully as many opposite-sex marriages. But what implications does that assertion have for the same-sex marriage debate as a whole?

Bennett argues that non-monogamous homosexual marriages will fatally undermine an already enfeebled institution. He makes this argument for one basic reason: men are naturally more promiscuous and male-male marriages will legitimize such promiscuity. But this argument has some problems. If you believe that men are naturally more promiscuous than women, then it follows that lesbian marriages will actually be more monogamous than heterosexual ones. So the alleged damage male-male marriages might do to heterosexual marriage would be countered by the good example that lesbian marriages would provide. It's a wash. And if you take the other conservative argument—that marriage exists not to reward monogamy but to encourage it—then Bennett is also in trouble. There is surely no group in society, by this logic, more in need of marriage rights than gay men. They are the group that most needs incentives for responsible behavior, monogamy, fidelity, and the like.

Putting Conditions on the Right to Marry

I'm not trying to be facetious here. The truth is, I think, marriage acts both as an incentive for virtuous behavior—and as a social blessing for the effort. In the past, we have wisely not made nitpicking assessments as to who deserves the right to marry and who does not. We have provided it to anyone prepared to embrace it and hoped for the best.

Imagine the consequences if you did otherwise. The government would spend its time figuring out whether certain groups of people were more or less capable of living up to the responsibilities of marriage

> *"If we're worried about polygamy, why not the threat of legally sanctioned necrophilia? Or bestiality?"*

and denying their right to it on that basis. The government might try to restrict it for more sexually active men under 20; or for women who have had an abortion. The government could argue, grotesquely, that because African Americans have, in general, higher illegitimacy rates, their right to marry should be abrogated. All these options rightly horrify us—but they are exactly the kind of conditions that Bennett and those who agree with him are trying to impose on gay citizens.

Or, in an equally troubling scenario, we could put conditions on the right to marry for certain individuals. People with a history of compulsive philandery in their relationships could be denied the right to marry; or people who have already failed at marriage once or twice or more; or people who are "free-riders" and marry late in life when the social sacrifice of marriage isn't quite so heavy. If we imposed these three restrictions, of course, three leading proponents of the Defense of Marriage Act would have their own right to marry taken away: chief-sponsor Congressman Bob Barr of Georgia (married three times), Bill Bennett (married at age 39) and Bill Clinton (ahem).

> *"The alleged damage male-male marriages might do to heterosexual marriage would be countered by the good example that lesbian marriages would provide."*

So how's this for a compromise: accept that human beings have natural, cultural and psychological differences. Accept that institutions can act both as incentives and rewards for moral behavior. Grant all citizens the same basic, civil institutions and hope that the mess and tragedy and joy of human life can somehow be sorted out for the better. That, after all, is what marriage does today for over 90 percent of the population. For some, it comes easily. For others, its commitments and responsibilities are crippling. But we do not premise the right to marry upon the ability to perform its demands flawlessly. We accept that human beings are variably virtuous, but that, as citizens, they should be given the same rights and responsibilities—period. That—and not the bogeymen of polygamy and adultery—is what the same-sex marriage debate is really about.

Same-Sex Marriage Would Be Good for Society

by William N. Eskridge Jr.

About the author: *William N. Eskridge Jr. is a professor at Georgetown Law Center in Washington, D.C., and the author of* The Case for Same-Sex Marriage.

Same-sex marriage is good for gay people and good for America, and for the same reason: It civilizes gays and it civilizes America.[1] Start with the former. For most of the twentieth century, lesbians, gay men, and bisexuals have been outlaws. The law relevant to us was the criminal code—not just sodomy prohibitions, which virtually defined us, but also disorderly conduct, lewdness, and vagrancy statutes, infractions of which led to employment and licensing penalties. The law relevant to us today is found in the civil code, most prominently in antidiscrimination statutes but increasingly in family law as well. Virtually no one in the gay and lesbian community would deny that this "civilizing" shift in the law reflects enormous progress and that such progress is incomplete until gay people enjoy the same rights and responsibilities as straight people. Marriage is the most important right the state has to offer, in part because being married entails dozens of associated rights, benefits, and obligations under state and federal law. As a formal matter, law's civilizing movement will not be complete until the same-sex married couple replaces the outlawed sodomite as the paradigmatic application of law to gay people.

Integration

Law's gradual decriminalization of homosexuality finds a parallel in gay lives. As we shed our outlaw status, we are increasingly integrated into (as opposed to being closeted from) the larger society and its spheres of business, re-

---

[1]My discussion in this and the next two paragraphs exploits the different meanings of *civilize* (all of which are found in unabridged dictionaries). As a law professor I naturally start with the strict legal meaning of *civilize*, namely, "changes from the criminal law to the civil law." This should be the least controversial (and admittedly pedantic) use of the term. The discussion immediately progresses to broader and more interesting meanings: "integrate into the law and customs of society" or simply "educate." I also use *civilize* in its most provocative sense: "tame" or "domesticate."

ligion, recreation, and education. Recognizing same-sex marriages would contribute to the integration of gay lives and the larger culture, to a nonlegal form of civilizing gays. Marriage would contribute to this integration because same-sex couples would be able to participate openly in this long-standing cultural institution. Such participation would establish another common tie between gay people and straight people. We are already coworkers, teachers, students, public officials, fellow worshippers, and parents; we share institutions of employment, religion, and education with the rest of the population. Once we are permitted to marry, we should also share the aspirations, joys, anxieties, and disappointments that straight couples find in matrimony. In time, moreover, same-sex marriage will likely contribute to the public acceptability of homosexual relationships. The interpersonal commitments entailed by same-sex marriages ought to help break down the stereotypes straights have about gays, especially about gay and bisexual men.

Lesbian and gay skeptics fear that civilizing gays would domesticate and tame us. This sort of fear is usually overstated, for same-sex couples do not simply ape the mores of traditional marriage. Indeed, the old-fashioned marriage of breadwinner husband and housekeeper wife cannot be replicated by same-sex couples; at least one of the husbands will be a housekeeper, and at least one of the wives will be a breadwinner. More important, a greater degree of domestication should not be rejected out of hand. Human history repeatedly testifies to the attractiveness of domestication born of interpersonal commitment, a signature of married life. It should not have required the AIDS epidemic to alert us to the problems of sexual promiscuity and to the advantages of committed relationships. In part because of their greater tendency toward bonding in committed pairs, lesbians have been the group least infected by the virus that leads to AIDS and have emerged in the 1990s as an unusually vital group. To the extent that males in our culture have been more sexually venturesome (more in need of civilizing), same-sex marriage could be a particularly useful commitment device for gay and bisexual men.

Since at least the nineteenth century, gay men have been known for their promiscuous subcultures. Promiscuity may be a consequence of biology (men may be naturally more promiscuous than women; if so, all-male couples would exaggerate this trait), or it may be the result of acculturation (the peculiar way Western society defines virility). In the world of

> *"Same-sex marriage is good for gay people and good for America, and for the same reason: It civilizes gays and it civilizes America."*

the closet, furtive behavior that is not only practically necessary but also addictively erotic may increase the likelihood of promiscuity. Whatever its source, sexual variety has not been liberating to gay men. In addition to the disease costs, promiscuity has encouraged a cult of youth worship and has contributed to the stereotype of homosexuals as people who lack a serious approach to life. (Indeed, a culture centered around nightclubs and bars is not one that can fundamentally satisfy the needs for connection and commitment that become more important as one grows older.) A self-reflective gay community ought to embrace marriage for its potentially civilizing effect on young and old alike.

Replacing Hatred with Acceptance

Same-sex marriage would also civilize Americans. Ours is a "creole" culture, created out of many constituent groups, each of which blends into the larger culture only after adding its own distinctive flavor. American society today is a synergy of Chinese, English, Mexican, Native American, Puerto Rican, African, Jewish, Japanese, Irish, Italian, Filipino, and *Gay* influences. Yet some segments of our society have at times militantly opposed some of these groups; witness our history of anti-Semitism, nativist sentiment against new immigrants, and interracial prejudice. Time after time, group hatred has been replaced by group acceptance and cooperation. Cooperating with others, people learn and grow. Our country has profited from the heterogeneity of the populace. The history we Americans point to with pride is a history of accommodation and inclusion. The history we Americans would rather forget, and should try to correct, is our history of prejudice and exclusion.

> *"This country would be . . . civilized . . . if it would end all vestiges of legal discrimination against its homosexual population."*

Gay people are neither an ethnic nor a racial group, but we are a group that has been traditionally excluded from equal rights in the United States. Our contributions have until recently been actively suppressed by laws that require or encourage us to remain closeted. This country would be edified—civilized, if you will—if it would end all vestiges of legal discrimination against its homosexual population. Essential to this project is the adoption of laws guaranteeing equal rights for lesbian and gay couples.

Bisexuals, gay men, and lesbians are citizens of the United States. Notwithstanding our ill treatment in the past, we love this country and have contributed in every way to its flourishing. A civilized polity assures equality for all its citizens. There can be no equality for lesbians, gay men, and bisexuals in the United States without same-sex marriage. This equality point has constitutional bite. The United States Supreme Court has repeatedly held that a civilized polity can only restrict the fundamental right to marry if there is a compelling reason to do so. The state cannot restrict the right to marry on the basis of punitive grounds or prejudice. For example, the Warren Court in 1967 struck down Virginia's law prohibiting people of different races from marrying. The Court did not dispute Virginia's claims that its citizens considered different-race marriages repulsive, contrary to their religious beliefs, and a threat to human genetic flourishing. The Court merely held that these beliefs do not justify limiting the fundamental right to marry. The Court's decision is in the best "live and let live" tradition of American law. The arguments rejected by the Court are eerily similar to those advanced by traditionalist opponents of same-sex marriage.

The Right to Marry

The Warren Court was not alone in protecting the right to marry. The Burger Court required states to permit remarriage of "deadbeat dads" in 1978. The Rehnquist Court in 1987 struck down a state's restrictions on marriage by prison inmates. The Court reasoned that prisoners have the same right to marry, to achieve the emotional, religious, and economic benefits of the institution, that other citizens have. The Court further held that restrictions on that right must be justified by something more than dislike of prisoners or generalized concerns about prison discipline. This unanimous decision reflects broader features of marriage law and suggests the civilizing consequences of recognizing same-sex marriage. In today's society the importance of marriage is relational and not procreational. . . .

When the state recognizes a couple's right to marry, it offers a recognition of the couple's citizenship, not a seal of approval for their lifestyle. Citizenship in a heterogeneous polity entails state tolerance of a variety of marriages, and states are not a bit choosy about who receives a marriage license. Convicted felons, divorced parents who refuse to pay child support, delinquent taxpayers, fascists, and communists—all receive marriage licenses from the state. The Supreme Court stands ready to discipline any state that denies these citizens their right to marry, yet no one believes that the license constitutes state approval of felony, default on support obligations, tax delinquency, communism, or fascism. People considered sexually deviant also routinely get marriage licenses. Pedophiles, transvestites, transsexuals, sadists, masochists, sodomites, and hermaphrodites can get marriage licenses in every state—so long as they can persuade the state that they are heterosexual pedophiles, transvestites, transsexuals, sadists, masochists, sodomites, and hermaphrodites (sometimes this is a pretty scholastic exercise). Gay people constitute virtually the only group in America whose members are not permitted to marry the partner they love. This is intolerable.

> *"State prohibitions against same-sex marriages may be antifamily and antichildren."*

Two Reasons

The state justifications for prohibiting same-sex marriage ultimately boil down to one negative reason and one positive reason. The negative reason is prejudice against lesbians, gay men, and bisexuals. As a matter of politics, homophobia is not a productive state policy, for it engenders a competition of spite and vengeance, the antithesis of a civilized polity. Civilizing America means taking homophobia off the national agenda—by constitutional decision making, if necessary. The positive reason for the prohibition is to foster family values in the state by reserving marriage for those who want to procreate and raise a family. This is a much more attractive value than homophobia, but *it does not support existing state bars to same-sex marriage.* Families are as heterogeneous as they are wonderful: they include couples with children, single mothers with children, grandparents with their grandchildren and a niece or nephew, and just couples. Families need not be heterosexual, and they need not procreate. The state has always allowed couples to marry even though they do not desire children or are physically incapable of procreation. Would anyone deny a marriage license to an octogenarian couple? Marriage in an urbanized society serves companionate, economic, and interpersonal goals that are independent of procreation, and the Supreme Court's most recent marriage decision (involving prisoners) reflects that reality. Civilizing America does not require that all couples have children.

Moreover many same-sex couples do have and raise children. Some bring children from prior marriages and relationships into the same-sex household. Lesbians have children through artificial insemination, and gay men have children through surrogacy and other arrangements. Same-sex couples can now adopt children in most states, and many take advantage of this opportunity. Every study that has been done of children raised in lesbian or gay households has found that the children have been raised well. Some studies have found that children of lesbian couples are better adjusted than children of single heterosexual mothers, presumably because there are two parents in the household. If this finding can be generalized, it yields the ironic point that state prohibitions against same-sex marriages may be antifamily and antichildren. The civilizing influence of family values, with or without children, may ultimately be the best argument for same-sex marriage.

Gay Marriage Would Not Harm Children

by April Martin

About the author: *April Martin, a psychologist, is the executive vice president of the Gay and Lesbian Parents Coalition International and the author of* The Lesbian and Gay Parenting Handbook.

The Hawaii legislature has directed the State's attorneys to use the "procreation" argument in their case against same-sex marriage: Since a man and a woman comprise the biological procreative unit, only heterosexual couples need the protection that marriage provides. [A Hawaiian trial court legalized same-sex marriage in December 1996.]

Four million lesbian and gay parents are dumbfounded. Are our eight million children not in need of protection?

Gays Are Parents

Same-sex couples are not biological procreative units, but they are nevertheless parents. They raise children in families where, most often, one parent is related only by devotion and hard work to the biological children of the other. The children rely on them, often calling both women "Mom," or both men "Dad." But because they can't get married, nonbiological parents feel the ever present danger that a court may not even view them as relevant parties in a custody decision if the biological parent should die or the relationship end in separation. And their children live with the ongoing insecurity that losing one parent in a tragedy might simultaneously mean losing their other parent in a courtroom.

In the summer of 1996, a Michigan court ignored the pleas of a nonbiological mother when the biological mother died of ovarian cancer. The judge even ignored the wishes of the two adolescent boys, raised for as long as they could remember by their two moms, and gave them instead to their biological father—a man who abandoned them until there were Social Security benefits to be had. If the women had been legally married, the court would have viewed her as a

From April Martin, "Same-Sex Marriage and Parenting," *GLPCI Network*, Fall 1996. Reprinted by permission of the author.

valid stepparent. As it was, her years of parenting didn't even merit visitation.

Child custody and visitation issues are the most frequent reasons that gays and lesbians go to court. In a system where unmarried couples are regarded as less stable than married couples, same-sex couples who would gladly get married if they could are dismissed for cohabiting without a license. Time after time we are told that we can't have custody of our children because we are not married. Now the State of Hawaii is saying that we can't get married because only heterosexuals need custody protection for their children. What's wrong with this picture?

"Not a single . . . research stud[y] . . . was able to find any detriment to children raised by same-sex parents."

My life partner and I, who have spent many thousands of dollars on a variety of side-door legal documents in an attempt to protect our children, continue to spend thousands more annually buying additional health insurance because without a marriage license we do not qualify for one family policy. Our children could have used that money for their education.

The State of Hawaii will maintain that heterosexual couples are the optimal units for raising children. Yet *Child Development*, the most prestigious peer-reviewed journal in its field, says that argument is completely unfounded. Not a single one of the several dozen legitimate research studies reviewed in a 1992 article was able to find any detriment to children raised by same-sex parents. Despite traditional gender hysteria that boys will somehow fail to be manly if raised by either no men or two men (huh?), the children studied turned out indistinguishable from those raised by heterosexual parents.

Meanwhile the adoption profession has become a significant supporter of gay and lesbian parents. They increasingly turn to same-sex couples to provide stable, loving homes for neglected, abandoned, and disabled children who would have nowhere else to go. I know same-sex parents raising children who were born crack addicted, children with AIDS, and children with severe cognitive challenges. Do these families not also deserve the protections that marriage provides?

Invisible Families

Unfortunately, our families are up against a serious adversary: invisibility. Those who know we exist still don't understand the discrimination we face.

We've had snippets of mainstream media recognition in the past decade, but gay and lesbian parents are still the least visible segment of the gay community. Media is understandably more excited by gender-bending, AIDS, and sexual explicitness. I have seen reporters' eyes glaze over when, hoping for the inside dope on our families, they hear, "Well, homework. Laundry. Struggles over eating vegetables." It doesn't make vivid copy.

Even the gay and lesbian movement has historically ignored us, buying into the idea that family issues are heterosexual issues. It is just now catching on that the freedom to define one's family is at the heart of the fight against gender-based discrimination.

And in the heterosexually dominated parenting world, gay and lesbian parents are barely detectable. Homophobia is still an acceptable hatred in the school systems. Teachers who would immediately step in to educate when a child uses racist or sexist epithets will allow kids in grade school to call each other "faggot" without saying a word. Millions of children are not yet safe enough to be able to say they are raised by two female or two male parents. Their nonbiological parents are often kept out of view—not brought to teacher conferences, not reported on family contact sheets, not mentioned except perhaps as Uncle Steve, or Mom's friend.

Legal marriage would not solve all the problems of homophobia for these families, but it would grant them sufficient safety to risk visibility. It would be far easier for a mother to say, "This is my wife and we are Alyssa's parents" than it is now for her to say, "This is my lesbian lover who lives with us." If parents can come out to teachers, pediatricians, school administrators, religious leaders, then those institutions will be empowered to protect children from homophobic assaults as well.

Same-sex marriage, at least for our era and culture, is change. It is the kind of change that remedies prior ignorance, and reflects a society's ability to mature and progress. As humans, we are generally inclined to greet change with anxiety. But those of us who are openly raising children as lesbian and gay parents probably know better than most that the cure for irrational fear is time and exposure.

When our children first went to school, the other kindergarten parents eyed us nervously. If you'd taken a poll that first week, they would have said "Oh, no" to the question of letting their children sleep at the house of lesbians. Our kids are adolescents now, and school friends with sleeping bags have been trooping through our kitchen for years. Some of those very same parents who once looked askance have become dear and trusted friends. Times change, people learn, and love is ultimately understood by all who care to listen. It is, after all, what makes a family.

Bibliography

Books

Henry J. Aaron,
Thomas E. Mann, and
Timothy Taylor, eds.
Values and Public Policy. Washington, DC: Brookings Institution, 1994.

Constance Ahrons
The Good Divorce: Keeping Your Family Together When Your Marriage Comes Apart. New York: HarperCollins, 1994.

Terry Arendell
Fathers and Divorce. Thousand Oaks, CA: Sage Publications, 1995.

Mary Kay Blakely
American Mom: Motherhood, Politics, and Humble Pie. Chapel Hill, NC: Algonquin Books, 1994.

David Blankenhorn
Fatherless America: Confronting Our Most Urgent Social Problem. New York: HarperPerennial, 1995.

Christopher Clulow, ed.
Women, Men, and Marriage. Northvale, NJ: Aronson, 1996.

Ellis Cose
A Man's World: How Real Is Male Privilege—and How High Is Its Price? New York: HarperCollins, 1995.

William N. Eskridge Jr.
The Case for Same-Sex Marriage: From Sexual Liberty to Civilized Commitment. New York: Free Press, 1996.

George Feifer
Divorce: An Oral Portrait. New York: New Press, 1995.

Debra Friedman
Towards a Structure of Indifference: The Social Origins of Maternal Custody. New York: Aldine de Gruyter, 1995.

Maggie Gallagher
The Abolition of Marriage: How We Destroy Lasting Love. Washington, DC: Regnery, 1996.

Carla B. Garrity and
Mitchell A. Baris
Caught in the Middle: Protecting the Children of High-Conflict Divorce. New York: Lexington Books, 1994.

John Mordechai
Gottman
What Predicts Divorce? The Relationship Between Marital Processes and Marital Outcomes. Hillsdale, NJ: Lawrence Erlbaum, 1994.

Shere Hite
The Hite Report on the Family: Growing Up Under Patriarchy. New York: Grove Press, 1994.

Penny Kaganoff and
Susan Spano, eds.
Women on Divorce: A Bedside Companion. New York: Harcourt Brace, 1995.

179

Bibliography

Karen Kayser — *When Love Dies: The Process of Marital Disaffection.* New York: Guilford Press, 1993.

Richard A. Mackey and Bernard A. O'Brien — *Lasting Marriages: Men and Women Growing Together.* Westport, CT: Praeger, 1995.

Charlotte Mayerson — *Goin' to the Chapel: Dreams of Love, Realities of Marriage.* New York: BasicBooks, 1996.

Michael J. McManus — *Marriage Savers: Helping Your Friends and Family Avoid Divorce.* Grand Rapids, MI: Zondervan, 1995.

David Popenoe — *Life Without Father: Compelling New Evidence That Fatherhood and Marriage Are Indispensable for the Good of Children and Society.* New York: Martin Kessler, 1996.

David Popenoe, Jean Bethke Elshtain, and David Blankenhorn, eds. — *Promises to Keep: Decline and Renewal of Marriage in America.* Lanham, MD: Rowman & Littlefield, 1996.

Andrew Sullivan — *Virtually Normal: An Argument About Homosexuality.* New York: Knopf, 1995.

Judith S. Wallerstein and Sandra Blakeslee — *The Good Marriage: How and Why Love Lasts.* New York: Houghton Mifflin, 1995.

Michele Weiner-Davis — *Divorce Busting: A Revolutionary and Rapid Program for Staying Together.* New York: Simon & Schuster, 1993.

Periodicals

Constance Ahrons — Symposium: "Should Government's Bias Against Marriage Be Reversed? No: Trying to Turn Back the Clock Won't Meet the Needs of Families," *Insight*, April 15, 1996. Available from 3600 New York Ave. NE, Washington, DC 20002.

Paul Akers — "Deadbeat Dads, Meet Your Counterparts: Walkaway Wives," *American Enterprise*, May/June 1996.

Brad Andrews — "A Singular Experience," *Newsweek*, May 10, 1993.

Hadley Arkes — "Odd Couples," *National Review*, August 12, 1996.

Alan AtKisson — "What Makes Love Last?" *New Age Journal*, September/October 1994.

Janet Scott Barlow — "Habla Therapy?" *Chronicles*, October 1996. Available from 934 N. Main St., Rockford, IL 61103.

David Blankenhorn — "Pay, Papa, Pay," *National Review*, April 3, 1995.

Center for Marriage and Family at Creighton University — "What Is Effective Marriage Preparation?" *Origins*, December 7, 1995. Available from 3211 4th St. NE, Washington, DC 20017-1100.

Nadine Cohodas — "Child Support: No More Pretty Please," *Governing*, October 1993.

Marriage and Divorce

David Orgon Coolidge — "The Dilemma of Same-Sex Marriage," *Crisis*, July/August 1996. Available from PO Box 10559, Riverton, NJ 08076-0559.

Lynda Dickson — "The Future of Marriage and Family in Black America," *Journal of Black Studies*, vol. 23, no. 4, June 1993. Available from 2455 Teller Rd., Thousand Oaks, CA 91320.

David Frum — "The Courts, Gay Marriage, and the Popular Will," *Weekly Standard*, September 30, 1996. Available from PO Box 710, Radnor, PA 19088-0710.

Maggie Gallagher — "Monogamy: The Cost of Disregarding the Real Meaning of Marriage," *Destiny*, January 1996. Available from 18398 Redwood Hwy., Selma, OR 97538.

Maggie Gallagher — Symposium: "Should Government's Bias Against Marriage Be Reversed? Yes: Welfare Reform and Tax Incentives Can Reverse the Antimarriage Tilt," *Insight*, April 15, 1996.

Dick Hart — "Real Men Don't Pay Alimony," *Harper's Magazine*, June 1993.

Datina M. Herd — "Unsupported Support," *Newsweek*, April 22, 1996.

Mary Ann Hogan — "The Good Marriage?" *Mother Jones*, July/August 1995.

Issues and Controversies on File — "Same-Sex Marriage," April 19, 1996. Available from 460 Park Ave. S, New York, NY 10016 7382.

Sandra Jacobson — "Restricting Divorce Hurts Children and Women," *New York Times*, February 21, 1996.

Dirk Johnson — "Attacking No-Fault Notion: Conservatives Try to Put Blame Back in Divorce," *New York Times*, February 12, 1996.

Fenton Johnson — "Wedded to an Illusion," *Harper's Magazine*, November 1996.

James Kunen — "Hawaiian Courtship," *Time*, December 16, 1996.

Kim Lawton — "'No-Fault' Divorce Under Assault," *Christianity Today*, April 8, 1996

Felicia Lee — "Influential Study on Divorce's Impact Is Said to Be Flawed," *New York Times*, May 9, 1996.

John Leland — "Tightening the Knot," *Newsweek*, February 19, 1996.

Michael J. McManus — "Become a Marriage Saver," *Focus on the Family,* July 1996. Available from PO Box 35500, Colorado Springs, CO 80935-3550.

Laura Mansnerus — "The Divorce Backlash," *Working Woman*, February 1995.

New York Times — "Lesbianism Does Not Bar Child Custody, Court Rules," June 22, 1994.

Katha Pollitt — "Subject to Debate," *Nation*, January 30, 1995.

Jane Bryant Quinn — "Sauce for the Goose," *Newsweek*, January 25, 1993.

Bibliography

Hanna Rosin	"Separation Anxiety," *New Republic*, May 6, 1996.
Gabriel Rotello	"To Have and to Hold," *Nation*, June 24, 1996.
Jim Ryun and Anne Ryun	"Courtship Makes a Comeback," *Focus on the Family*, November 1995.
K.C. Scott	"'Mom, I Want to Live with My Boyfriend,'" *Reader's Digest*, February 1994.
Glenn Stanton	"The Counter-Revolution Against Easy Divorce," *American Enterprise*, May/June 1996.
Andrew Sullivan	"Hawaiian Aye," *New Republic*, December 30, 1996.
U.S. News & World Report	"Should Gay Marriage Be Legal?" June 3, 1996.
David Van Biema	"Dunning Deadbeats," *Time*, April 3, 1995.
Judith Wallerstein and Sandra Blakeslee	"Happily Ever After," *Family Therapy Networker*, November/December 1995. Available from 8528 Bradford Rd., Silver Spring, MD 20910.
James Q. Wilson	"Against Homosexual Marriage," *Commentary*, March 1996.

Organizations to Contact

The editors have compiled the following list of organizations concerned with the issues debated in this book. The descriptions are derived from materials provided by the organizations. All have publications or information available for interested readers. The list was compiled on the date of publication of the present volume; names, addresses, phone numbers, and e-mail/Internet addresses may change. Be aware that many organizations may take several weeks or longer to respond to inquiries, so allow as much time as possible.

American Civil Liberties Union (ACLU)
Lesbian and Gay Rights/AIDS Project
132 W. 43rd St.
New York, NY 10036
(212) 944-9800
fax: (212) 869-9065
Internet: http://www.aclu.org

The ACLU is the nation's oldest and largest civil liberties organization. Its Lesbian and Gay Rights/AIDS Project, started in 1986, handles litigation, education, and public-policy work on behalf of gays and lesbians. It supports same-sex marriage. The ACLU publishes the monthly newsletter *Civil Liberties Alert,* the handbook *The Rights of Lesbians and Gay Men,* the briefing paper "Lesbian and Gay Rights," and the book *The Rights of Families: The Basic ACLU Guide to the Rights of Today's Family Members.*

Children's Rights Council (CRC)
220 I St. NE, Suite 230
Washington, DC 20002-4362
(202) 547-6227
(800) 787-KIDS
fax: (202) 546-4272

The CRC is concerned with the healthy development of children of divorced and separated parents. Its efforts are concentrated on strengthening marriage, reforming child custody laws, minimizing hostilities between separated or divorced parents, and advocating for a child's right to grow up in a healthy family environment. The council publishes the quarterly newsletter *Speak Out for Children.*

Concerned Women for America (CWA)
370 L'Enfant Promenade SW, Suite 800
Washington, DC 20024
(202) 488-7000
fax: (202) 488-0806

The CWA is an educational and legal defense foundation that seeks to strengthen the traditional family by applying Judeo-Christian moral standards. It opposes gay marriage and the granting of additional civil rights protections to gays and lesbians. It publishes the monthly magazine *Family Voice* and various position papers on gay marriage and other issues.

Family Research Council
801 G St. NW
Washington, DC 20001
(202) 393-2100
fax: (202) 393-2134
Internet: http://www.frc.org

The council is a research, resource, and educational organization that promotes the traditional family, which the council defines as a group of people bound by marriage, blood, or adoption. The council opposes gay marriage, adoption rights, and no-fault divorce. It publishes numerous reports from a conservative perspective on issues affecting the family, including "Free to Be Family." Among its other publications are the monthly newsletter *Washington Watch* and the bimonthly journal *Family Policy.*

Family Research Institute (FRI)
PO Box 62640
Colorado Springs, CO 80962
(303) 681-3113

FRI distributes information about family, sexual, and substance abuse issues. The institute believes that strengthening marriage would reduce many social problems, including crime, poverty, and sexually transmitted diseases. FRI publishes the bimonthly newsletter *Family Research Report* as well as the position paper "What's Wrong with Gay Marriage?"

Fathers for Equal Rights
PO Box 010847, Flagler Station
Miami, FL 33101
(305) 895-6351
(305) 895-7461

Fathers for Equal Rights is a fathers support and self-help group and has been a child custody clearinghouse since 1967. It also advocates for fathers' rights in family court. The organization publishes several manuals and self-help guides, such as *Winning Child Custody Cases* and *Fathers' and Mothers' Guide to Child Custody Dispute.*

Focus on the Family
8605 Explorer Dr.
Colorado Springs, CO 80920
(719) 531-3400

Focus on the Family is a Christian organization that seeks to strengthen the traditional family in America. It believes the family is the most important social unit and maintains that reestablishing the traditional two-parent family will end many social problems. In addition to conducting research and educational programs, Focus on the Family publishes the monthly periodical *Focus on the Family* and the reports "Setting the Record Straight: What Research *Really* Says About the Consequences of Homosexuality," "No-Fault Fallout: Finding Fault with No-Fault Divorce," "Only a Piece of Paper? The Unquestionable Benefits of Lifelong Marriage," and "Twice as Strong: The Undeniable Advantages of Raising Children in a Traditional Two-Parent Family."

The Heritage Foundation
214 Massachusetts Ave. NE
Washington, DC 20002
(202) 546-4400
fax: (202) 546-0904

The Heritage Foundation is a public-policy research institute that promotes limited government and the free-market system. The foundation publishes monographs, books, and papers, such as the articles "A Mom and Pop Manifesto: What the Pro-Family Movement Wants from Congress," "Prodigal Dad: How We Bring Fathers Home to Their Children," and "Split Personality: Why Aren't Conservatives Talking About Divorce?" It also publishes the weekly *Backgrounder* and the quarterly journal *Policy Review*.

Institute for American Values
1841 Broadway, Suite 211
New York City, NY 10023
(212) 246-3942
fax: (212) 541-6665

The institute is a research organization that focuses on issues affecting the well-being of families and children in the United States. It publishes the report "Marriage in America: A Report to the Nation," the papers "Beyond the Murphy Brown Debate: Ideas for Family Policy," "Marriage, Parenting, and Women's Quest for Equality," and "The Family Values of Americans," and the books *Fatherless America* and *Life Without Father*.

IntiNet Resource Center
PO Box 4322
San Rafael, CA 94913
(415) 507-1739
e-mail: pad@well.com

The center promotes nonmonogamous relationships as an alternative to the traditional family. It also serves as a clearinghouse for information on nonmonogamous relationships and as a network for people interested in alternative family lifestyles. IntiNet publishes the quarterly newsletter *Floodtide,* the book *Polyamory: The New Love Without Limits,* and the *Resource Guide for the Responsible Non-Monogamist.*

Loving More
PO Box 4358
Boulder, CO 80306
(303) 543-7540
e-mail: ryam@lovemore.com
Internet: http://www.lovemore.com

Loving More explores and supports many different forms of family and relationships, such as open marriage, extended family, and multi-partner marriages. It also serves as a national clearinghouse for the multi-partner movement. The organization publishes the quarterly magazine *Loving More.*

Men's Rights (MR)
PO Box 163180
Sacramento, CA 95816
(916) 484-7333

MR believes that divorce and custody laws oppress and dehumanize men and keep them away from their families. It seeks to end sexism by extending the right of nurturing and raising children to men. MR publishes position papers on divorce and custody as well as the newsletter *New Release.*

National Council on Family Relations (NCFR)
3989 Central Ave. NE, Suite 550
Minneapolis, MN 55421
(612) 781-9331
fax: (612) 781-9348

The council is an organization of social workers, clergy, counselors, psychologists, and others who research in fields such as education, social work, psychology, sociology, home economics, anthropology, and health care. NCFR publishes the quarterly *Journal of Marriage and Family Relations* and *Family Relations.*

National Gay and Lesbian Task Force (NGLTF)
2320 17th St. NW
Washington, DC 20009-2702
(202) 332-6483
fax: (202) 332-0207

The NGLTF is a civil rights advocacy organization that lobbies Congress and the White House on a range of civil rights and AIDS issues affecting gays and lesbians. The organization is working to make same-sex marriage legal. It publishes numerous papers and pamphlets, the booklet *To Have and to Hold: Organizing for Our Right to Marry,* the fact sheet "Lesbian and Gay Families," the quarterly *NGLTF Newsletter,* and the monthly *Activist Alert.*

The Rockford Institute
Center on the Family in America
934 N. Main St.
Rockford, IL 61103
(815) 964-5811
fax: (815) 965-1826

The institute works to return America to Judeo-Christian values and supports traditional roles for men and women. Its Center on the Family in America studies the evolution of the family and the effects of divorce on society. The institute publishes the newsletter *Main Street Memorandum* and the monthly periodicals *Family in America* and *Chronicles.*

Traditional Values Coalition
139 C St. SE
Washington, DC 20003
(202) 547-8570
fax: (202) 546-6403

The coalition strives to restore what the group believes are the traditional moral and spiritual values in American government, schools, media, and society. It believes that gay marriage threatens the family unit and extends civil rights beyond what the coalition considers appropiate limits. The coalition publishes the quarterly newsletter *Traditional Values Report* as well as various information papers addressing same-sex marriage and other issues.

Index

8/99 (5) 8/99
7/01 (6) 12/99
9/03 (7) 5/03
9/05 (8) 4/04
8/08 (9) 4/08
9/15 (15) 3/15